INTERNATIONAL
WRITERS CENTER
SERIES
William H. Gass
and
Lorin Cuoco,
Series Editors

The
WRITER
in
POLITICS

Edited by William H. Gass *and* Lorin Cuoco

SOUTHERN ILLINOIS UNIVERSITY PRESS
Carbondale and Edwardsville

Library of Congress Cataloging-in-Publication Data

The writer in politics / edited by William H. Gass and Lorin Cuoco.
    p. cm. — (International Writers Center Series)
    Papers and ensuing discussion from a conference held Oct. 18–21,
1992, Washington University, St Louis, Mo.
    Contents: The writer and politics: a litany / William H. Gass —
The book show / Antonio Skármeta — Politics and literature : the
odd couple / Mario Vargas Llosa — Trying to breathe / Luisa
Valenzuela — Savaging the soul of a nation / Nuruddin Farah —
The poetry of witness / Carolyn Forché — Cold turkey / Breten
Breytenbach.
    Includes bibliographical references.
    1. Politics and literature.   2. Politics in literature.   I. Gass,
William H., 1924– .   II. Cuoco, Lorin, 1954– .   III. Series.
PN51.W724   1996
809′.93358—dc20   95-45539
    ISBN 0-8093-2050-9   CIP

These authors' essays appeared in slightly different form in the following
    publications:
Breyten Breytenbach, "Why Are Writers Always the Last to Know?" *New
    York Times Book Review*, March 28, 1993.
Nuruddin Farah, "Savaging the Soul of a Nation," *In These Times*,
    vol. 17, no. 3, December 28, 1992.
Mario Vargas Llosa, "The Real Life of the Latin American Novelist,"
    Harper's Magazine, vol. 287, no. 1720, September 1993.

The paper used in this publication meets the minimum requirements of
American National Standard for Information Sciences—Permanence of
Paper for Printed Library Materials, ANSI Z39.48-1984. ∞

Contents

Contents

Preface

The International Writers Center was established at Washington University in St. Louis in October 1990 with William H. Gass as director and me as associate director. It is not clear if the idea for it was like the conception, development, and birth of the skyscraper, that is, a construct simultaneously deliberated upon by many in disparate redoubts, but it grew up on the brink of a boom whose benefits include a renascent interest in writing, which we romantically hope means a renewed interest in reading. Something happened and not just in St. Louis. And it is still going on now, as writers centers, writers groups, open mike nights, and bookstore competition grow like so much *pilobolus*.

The Writer in Politics conference was presented at Washington University, October 18–21, 1992, with two panel discussions during the day and literary readings at night. Each day was devoted to one part of the theme: the Writer in Politics, the Writer under a Politics, the Writer with a Politics. What follows are the six essays composed for this conference, as well as the transcriptions of the panelists' and audience members' responses. There is a companion volume published by *New Letters* (vol. 58, no. 4) featuring writers who wrote on this subject.

This book would not have been possible without the transcribing powers of Mira Tanna who got it all, down to the stage directions. She captured the ether and put it on paper. Were I able, I would canonize her.

I am also grateful for the editorial assistance of Melissa Aptman, Ethan Bumas, Diana Kasdan, Anne Kemerer, and Kim Ketive, and to María Inés Lagos and Randolph Pope for expert consultation.

Without the writers, there would have been no conference. We are grateful to the six essayists and to the panelists for their contributions.

Without a conference, there would have been no book. We are indebted to the Harry Edison Foundation, the Missouri Arts Council, the Regional Arts Commission, and the contributing university departments for financial support.

Without Gerhild Williams, associate provost of Washington University, there would be no International Writers Center. We are profoundly grateful to William H. Danforth, chancellor of Washington University from 1970 to 1995, who said yes.

LORIN CUOCO

Contributors

Essayists

Breyten Breytenbach was born in Bonnievale, Cape Province, South Africa, on September 16, 1939. He began writing poetry in Afrikaans while studying at the University of Cape Town. In 1959, Breytenbach left South Africa for Europe, settling in France. Breytenbach became known first as a painter, exhibiting his work in Europe and America. Soon he became known for his writings, too, winning the Afrikaans Press Prize for his first volume of poetry, *The Iron Cow Must Sweat*, published in 1964. He and his Vietnamese wife made arrangements to return to South Africa to receive the award, but they were denied visas because of their interracial marriage, illegal under South African law. Finally, in 1973, they were issued a three-month visa. This visit inspired Breytenbach's book, *A Season in Paradise* (1976), which describes a journey to his homeland and an interior journey into his youth. A vehement critic of apartheid, Breytenbach entered the country illegally in 1975 to recruit new members to Okhela, a clandestine organization of non-Communist white South African exiles. He was arrested and convicted under the Terrorist Act and sentenced to nine years in jail. He was released seven years later and exiled from South Africa. He wrote about his experiences in prison in *The True Confessions of an Albino Terrorist* (1983) and *Mouroir: Mirrornotes of a Novel* (1984). Since the demise of apartheid, Breytenbach has been able to travel to South Africa. He divides his time between Paris, Spain, and Senegal, where he works with the Gorée Institute to build democratic institutions in Africa.

Breytenbach is the only South African to win the South African Central News Agency award five times, for *The House of the Deaf* (1967), *Gangrene* (1969), *Lotus* (1970), *Eclipse* (1983), and *Memory of Snow and Dust* (1989). He was also awarded the Pier Paolo Pasolini Prize for Literature. His other works that have been translated into English include *Sinking Ship Blues* (1977), *And Death as White as*

Words (1978), *In Africa Even the Flies Are Happy* (1978), *End Papers* (1986), *Judas Eye and Self-Portrait/Deathwatch* (1988), *All One Horse: Fictions and Images* (1990), and *Return to Paradise* (1994).

Nuruddin Farah was born in Baidoa, Somalia, in 1945. His first novel, *From a Crooked Rib* (1970), was the first work of fiction to be published by a Somali writer in English. His next work, *A Naked Needle*, was published in 1976. Farah's novels, *Sweet and Sour Milk* (1981), *Sardines* (1980), and *Close Sesame* (1983) make up the trilogy, *Variations on the Theme of an African Dictatorship*. *Maps* (1986) is set in modern Africa and explores the anguish of those living on a continent where national boundaries have been drawn by foreign hands.

Farah has been recognized internationally for his writing. *Sweet and Sour Milk* won the English-Speaking Union Literary Award of 1980. He received the Swedish Tucholsky Literary Award given to literary exiles in 1991. He received Zimbabwe's Best Novel of the Year Award for his book *Gifts*, published in 1993. Farah has taught at the University of Mogadishu and has been a guest professor at the University of Minnesota, State University of New York at Stony Brook, Brown University, the University of Bayreuth, the University of London, Makerere University, and the University of Khartoum. He lives in Kaduna, Nigeria.

Carolyn Forché was born in Detroit, Michigan, in 1950. She received degrees from Michigan State University and Bowling Green University. In 1977 with a Guggenheim Foundation fellowship, Forché traveled to El Salvador. Her experiences there led to her second book of poetry, *The Country Between Us*, published in 1982. She has been active in human rights organizations such as Amnesty International and PEN, and has served on the Commission on United States–Central American Relations. She edited a collection of poetry by writers who have borne witness to political repression entitled *Against Forgetting: Twentieth Century Poetry of Witness*, published in 1993.

Forché's first collection of poems, *Gathering the Tribes*, published in 1976, won the Yale Series of Younger Poets Award. *The Country Between Us* was chosen as the Lamont Selection of the Academy of American Poets. She has received fellowships from the National Endowment for the Arts and the Lannan Foundation. Forché has served as a visiting lecturer at Vassar College and at Brandeis, New York, and Columbia Universities. She teaches at George Mason University in Virginia. Her latest book of poetry is *The Angel of History*, published in 1994.

Antonio Skármeta was born in 1940 in Antofagasta, Chile. He studied philosophy at the University of Chile and received his master's degree from Columbia University in New York. Skármeta has taught at the University of Chile in Santiago, the School for Journalism at the Catholic University of Chile, and the German Academy of Cinema and Television; he teaches every other year in the Department of Romance Languages and Literatures at Washington University in St. Louis. He has been cultural editor of the magazines *Ercilla*, *Ahora*, and *La Quinta Rueda* in Santiago. In 1975, Skármeta accepted an invitation from the Office of Academic Interchange's Arts Program to emigrate to West Berlin, where he worked as an independent writer until the restoration of democracy in Chile. After returning to Chile in 1989, he cofounded and hosted the television show "El Show de los Libros" (The book show). He now lives in Santiago.

El entusiasmo (Enthusiasm), his first book, was published in 1967. Skármeta's short story collection, *Desnudo en el Tejado* (Naked on the roof), was awarded the House of the Americas Prize in 1969. He wrote his first screenplay, *La Victoria*, in 1972, and directed his first film in 1982, an adaptation of his novel *Burning Patience*, which was published in the United States in 1987. His novel about the Nicaraguan Revolution, *Insurrection*, was published in 1982; he has written about his own country in *I Dreamt the Snow Was Burning*, published in 1985. Skármeta also has received recognition from the European Broadcasting Union for the radio play *La Búsqueda* (The search), several honorable mentions for the Prix Italia, and countless prizes from international film festivals. His television show has been recognized as the Best Television Program of the Year. His other works in English include *Chileno!* (1979), *Stories* (1991), and *Watch Where the Wolf Is Going* (1991).

Luisa Valenzuela was born in Buenos Aires, Argentina, on November 26, 1938, the daughter of Argentine writer Luisa Mercedes Levinson. At an early age, Luisa Valenzuela began writing for the magazine *Quince Abriles*. She worked with Jorge Luis Borges at the

National Library of Argentina. In 1958, Valenzuela traveled to Paris as a correspondent for *El Mundo*, an Argentine daily newspaper. She returned to Buenos Aires in 1961 to write for Argentina's foremost newspaper *La Nación*. She attended the University of Iowa Writers' Workshop as a Fulbright Fellow in 1969.

In her books, Valenzuela has addressed the military dictatorship that ruled Argentina from 1976 to 1983. In *Strange Things Happen Here* (1979), she used humor, the absurd, and the grotesque to break through the barriers of censorship in an increasingly violent country. After realizing that she could not fight back against the regime, she left the country in 1979. Ten years later, she returned to Buenos Aires, after the restoration of democracy. Shocked by the existence of remnants of the former military regime, she wrote *Bedside Manners*, published in 1994.

She has been a Guggenheim Fellow, Writer-in-Residence at Columbia University, and a fellow of the New York Institute for the Humanities. Her other works published in the United States include *Clara* (1976), *The Lizard's Tail* (1983), *Other Weapons* (1985), *He Who Searches* (1986), *Open Door* (1988), *The Censors* (1992), and *Black Novel with Argentines* (1992).

Mario Vargas Llosa was born in Arequipa, Peru, on March 28, 1936. He received his bachelor's degree at the University of San Marcos in Lima and in 1958 won a scholarship to the University of Madrid. In 1959, he was awarded the Leopoldo Alas prize for his book of short stories *Los jefes* (*The Cubs and Other Stories*). After completing his studies in Madrid, he lived in Paris for fifteen years where he worked as a journalist for France Press Agency and later for French Radio and Television. In 1963, he published his first novel, *La ciudad y los perros* (published in the United States in 1966 as *The Time of the Hero*), which satirized the military academy he attended in Lima. Copies of the book were publicly burned by officials of this school. The book was awarded the Biblioteca Breve prize in Spain and received second place for the French Prix Formentor. His second novel, *La casa verde* (*The Green House*), published in 1968, was awarded literary prizes in Peru and Venezuela.

Many of Vargas Llosa's works criticize the Peruvian social and political system. The novel *Captain Pantoja and the Special Service*

(1978) is a farcical portrayal of a military brothel in the Peruvian Amazon while *Conversation in the Cathedral* (1984) explores the hypocrisy and corruption of Peruvian business and politics.

Vargas Llosa served as president of PEN from 1976 to 1979 and headed the commission appointed by the Peruvian government to investigate the massacre of eight journalists in the Andes in 1983. In 1988, he started Libertad, the political party that had its first congress in 1989. He ran unsuccessfully for president of Peru in 1990. He wrote about his political experiences in *A Fish in the Water* (1994). His other works that have been translated into English include *Aunt Julia and the Scriptwriter* (1982), *The War of the End of the World* (1984), *The Perpetual Orgy: Flaubert and Madame Bovary* (1986), *The Real Life of Alejandro Mayta* (1986), *The Storyteller* (1986), *Who Killed Palomino Molero?* (1987), *Three Plays: Young Lady from Tacna, Kathie and the Hippopotamus, and La Chunga* (1990), *In Praise of the Stepmother* (1990), *A Writer's Reality* (1991), *Fiction: The Power of Lies* (1993), and *Literature and Freedom* (1994). His play *The Madman of the Balconies* was produced in London in 1993. Mario Vargas Llosa lives in Europe.

Panelists

Eavan Boland has written seven books of poetry including *Outside History* and *In a Time of Violence*. She is the author of *Object Lessons: The Life of the Woman and the Poet in Our Time*. She resides in Dublin, Ireland.

Marc Chénetier is a professor of American literature at l'Ecole Normale Supérieure in Paris and has translated numerous American authors, including William H. Gass, into French.

Robert Coover is writer-in-residence at Brown University. He is the author of *Origin of the Brunists, Pricksongs & Descants, A Public Burning,* and *Gerald's Party*. His latest work is *Pinocchio in Venice*.

Wayne Fields is dean of University College and a professor of English at Washington University. He is the author of *What the River Knows: An Angler in Mid-Stream* and *The Past Leads a Life of its Own.*

William H. Gass, director of the International Writers Center, is David May Distinguished University Professor in the Humanities at Washington University. He has written several books of fiction and essays including *In the Heart of the Heart of the Country* and *The Habitations of the Word*, the National Book Critics Circle Award winner for Criticism in 1985. His novel *The Tunnel* was published in 1995.

Robert Hegel has served as chair of the Department of Asian and Near Eastern Languages and Literatures at Washington University. He has written and edited books on both modern and imperial Chinese literature.

Ron Himes is the founder of the St. Louis Black Repertory Company, which produces works of African American and Third World playwrights. He is an adjunct professor of African and Afro-American Studies at Washington University.

María Inés Lagos is an associate professor of Spanish at Washington University.

Liu Binyan worked as a special correspondent for China's official newspaper, *The People's Daily*. He has written a book of essays, *China's Crisis, China's Hope*, and a memoir, *A Higher Kind of Loyalty*.

Janet Majerus is the mayor of University City, Missouri, and author of the novel *Grandpa and Frank*, which was made into a television special called "Home to Stay."

William Matheson is a professor of comparative literature and director of Graduate Studies in Chinese, Japanese, and Comparative Literature at Washington University.

James McLeod is dean of the College of Arts and Sciences at Washington University. He has served as director of African and Afro-American Studies and is a professor of German.

Steven Meyer is an assistant professor of English at Washington University.

Eric Pankey directs the Writing Program at Washington University and has written four books of poetry, including *Apocrypha* and *Reliquary World*.

Margaret Sayers Peden is a professor emerita of Spanish at the University of Missouri, Columbia, and has translated works by Carlos Fuentes, Octavio Paz, Isabel Allende, Juan Rulfo, Ernesto Sábato, and Pablo Neruda into English.

Joe Pollack is a journalist with the *St. Louis Post-Dispatch*.

Randolph Pope chairs the Committee on Comparative Literature and is a professor of Spanish at Washington University.

Anton Shammas is the author of three books of poetry, a children's book, and the novel *Arabesques*, the only book of his to be translated from the Hebrew into English.

Richard Watson is a professor in the Department of Philosophy at Washington University and the author of *The Philosopher's Diet*, *The Philosopher's Joke*, and *The Philosopher's Demise: Learning French*. His latest novel is *Niagara*.

I

Introduction

1   The Writer in Politics: A Litany

William H. Gass

ocrates was accused and convicted of corrupting the youth. His enemies said he believed in gods other than the gods of the state. It would become a convenient charge, a familiar crime. And Socrates hadn't written a word, though he would inspire some. Plato got even by banishing most poets from his ideal Republic (a gesture whose import was so theoretical it failed to unkilter a single rhyme); for, after all, if the poets had not actually invented all the gods, they had certainly assigned them their places in the Olympian hierarchy, and written their roles in the sordid tales that were to be their myths. How should one punish such offenses: to have invented gods who do not exist, or written lies about those who do? We are all prepared to applaud eloquence when it is employed in the service of truth, but when it is turned the other way, should we continue to admire it anyway—although now as the display of splendid technique and an instance of inspired rodomontade?

Sir Thomas Malory was a parliamentarian before he became a crook. He was charged with robbing churches, with extortion, with rape, and was jailed nine times by our least numerous count. During his idle days of imprisonment he penned what became the *Book of King Arthur and his Noble Knights of the Round Table*. Evil to the end, he cribbed its people, plots, and their unfolding, from previous romances. Ditto a lot of that for O. Henry. François Villon was par-

doned, fled town until he felt his crimes were forgotten, or otherwise
escaped incarceration for brawling, burglary, petty theft, and fatally
wounding a priest, finally disappearing altogether, probably a good
idea. Benvenuto Cellini waited until the arrival of old age, another
kind of prison, before writing his autobiography; but he was quar-
relsome in his youth, and murdered at least two men before fame
eased him into innocence. Giovanni Casanova de Seingalt likewise
led a life of interesting dubiety—gambling, whoring, spying, dup-
ing, playing with black magic—until the heretical presuppositions
of his illicit spells clapped him in prison. His dramatic escape paral-
lels the earlier feats of Cellini, and gave him even more to brag
about.

The Charterhouse of Parma, one of the great political novels, nevertheless turns on nothing more political than love. Here the prison
romance is carried to new heights, namely to the top of the three-
hundred-foot Farnese Tower, where, in its more elevated cell, Stendhal's
Italian tenor-like hero, Fabrizio del Dongo, has been unjustly confined,
almost as Cellini was in Castel Sant' Angelo, or like the novel's more
explicit model, Alessandro Farnese, who escaped from such a tower by
means of a rope (as we like to measure things today) the length of a
football field. But lo! from his perch Fabrizio can glimpse the governor's
beautiful daughter who lives in an adjoining turret, and naturally he falls
in love, and refuses his opportunity for freedom because it would mean
losing sight of her. What woman could reject such devotion! But then!
she orders him to flee on her account, and thus Fabrizio begins his famous descent in pages through which one holds one's breath.

The notorious Marquis de Sade, who made libertinism a profession, passed twenty-seven years of his life in the lockup, where he
wrote most of the trash that made his name a Name. Brought up by
his uncle (a profligate Abbé), he was only months into his arranged
marriage when he was arrested for fanciful inventions at an orgy. Released, he began to misspend his wife's dowry, much of it on a little
house he had built for his debaucheries, the rest on a famous whore
he had taken as his mistress. He subsequently eloped with his wife's
sister, was condemned to death for poisoning and sodomy, and de-
bauched a servant girl whose father took a shot at him with an aim
unfortunately untrained. Frequently hunted by the police, he was
eventually imprisoned in the Bastille where he incited the people to
revolt by scattering notes from the window of his cell, and addressing

them through a funnel he devised to magnify his voice. We can get an idea of what he said by reading his "Address to the French Nation: Yet Another Effort, Frenchmen, If You Would Become Republicans." The unlucky marquis was transferred to an insane asylum only days before the Bastille was stormed and its prisoners released. For Sade, every sexual act was political, and buggery was simply a way of marking your ballot.

Marco Polo was made a prisoner of war by the Genovese, and it was in jail that he told his eventually famous tale to a fellow detainee who no doubt listened in Venetian but wrote down what he heard in French. Like so many flies, his merchant friends are alleged to have gathered around his death bed to beg him to erase those made-up miracles like gunpowder and paper money from his pages and take back his enticing lies. Ben Jonson contributed to the maintenance of artistic standards by killing an actor in a duel. Sharing similar values, the court let him off. Chaucer was a French prisoner of war before embarking on an extensive and successful public career: controller of customs, justice of the peace, clerk of the king's works, royal forester, member of Parliament. Frightened by hellfire and other unpleasant fates he felt awaited him, he cravenly disavowed his secular works. Similarly, a soldier, Charles d'Orléans was captured by the English at Agincourt. The Duke of Burgundy ransomed him after twenty-five years on the promise that Charles would marry his niece.

Miguel de Cervantes was captured by Turkish pirates and dungeoned in Algeria. Perhaps this rehearsal prepared him for his later incarceration for fraud. In any case, he began *Don Quixote* surrounded by thick walls and dim light. Sir Walter Raleigh suffered the disfavor of the court on three occasions. During his second stay in the Tower of London he completed the first volume of his *History of the World*, while during the third he lost his head. What he had written was never an issue. Thomas Wyatt also went often to visit that perilous Tower, though each time he was put in, a very well-placed lady got him out. John Bunyan was arrested for unlicensed preaching. During his first stint in prison he invented that great title, *Grace Abounding to the Chief of Sinners*, and then he even went on to write the book. During his second sentence, he began *Pilgrim's Progress*. George Chapman mocked the Scots and was jugged by James I, who was one of the Scots mocked. John Wilmot, the second earl of Rochester, was convicted of abduction, though he later made an honest woman of the heiress he had kidnapped, both marrying her and giving her three more children than he gave his mistress. Rochester misspent his life in a series of almost classical debaucheries. His cowardly repentance and religious conversion at the end did not save him from hell where, between moments of beautiful lamentation, we can be confident he is still burning.

Galileo experienced house arrest, and was also, though in different circumstances, compelled to recant, although he had attributed his work to a nom de plume. Boethius was arrested and executed in Pavia. Between these two events he wrote *De Consolatione Philosophiae*. One hopes his prescription worked for him. Descartes deemed it wise to delay publication of his quietly subversive books and to seek protection of powerful patrons, while moving about a lot. Spinoza was hounded for heresy, and a contract, it's said, put out on his life. It is doubtless small comfort to Salman Rushdie to have such distinguished company. Francis Bacon prosecuted his patron, Essex, for treason, and was found guilty, himself, of bribery and consequently expelled from court. Lucilio Vanini was burnt at the stake. (Only philosophers remember this.) Giordano Bruno suffered the same painful fate. Nothing was ever done to Louisa May Alcott. Aretino specialized in scurrilous libels, and he was thoroughly thrashed a few times by his enemies, but he was able to stink up his pages with happy impunity because he kept friends in high papal places, and aided many a scoundrel with his wealth. In short, he played politics, and sang the conniver's tunes. For his skills, the gods let his liver fail, and he died, they say, when a blood vessel burst in his throat while he was laughing at a bawdy joke. In sum, he had a good life, although he hardly led one.

Petronius did not have such luck. Falsely accused of treason, though guilty only of elegance and good taste, he was forced to open his own veins. Henry Howard, the Earl of Surrey, was also groundlessly accused of the same high crime, and despite a distinguished career of service in the military, he was executed on Tower Hill. However, George Villiers, the Duke of Buckingham, was a legitimately schemeful sort. An accomplished court intriguer, he shifted his weight like someone on a skateboard, and earned Dryden's description of him as a "chemist, fiddler, statesman, and buffoon." Thomas Hobbes and Edmund Waller were royalists or roundheads as the occasion required, proving once more that a cleverly managed lack of loyalty is like money in the bank. Edmund Burke, paymaster and member of Parliament, spent most of his life opposing not only revolutions but their causes. Although in and out of office, as politicians often are, and an accomplished maker of enemies, his eloquence was never interrupted, but grew admirably, although futilely, grander as more and more rebellions broke out despite his advice.

The Romans were hard on their heroes. Cicero was not particularly brave, but his words were, and it was for them that Mark Anthony had Cicero's head and hand nailed to the rostrum of the Forum. Mark Anthony still has his admirers, proving that nothing is unimaginable. Sir Charles Sedley was a retired rake who sat in Parliament and wrote love lyrics. His head remained firmly on. August Kotzebue, on the other hand, was always in hot water. Arrested as a German spy by Czar Paul I, and sent to Siberia, he was pardoned the next year and made director of the German theatre in St. Petersburg. A little while later, having turned his coat inside out, he returned to Germany as an agent of another czar, this time, Alexander I. His duties included editing a reactionary weekly in Mannheim; but—for such are the risks of extremism and notoriety—he was murdered by a member of a radical student movement. Among his other misfortunes, Kotzebue was married three times. Sarah Orne Jewett and Willa Cather were spared such indignities. However, Luis Vaz de Camoëns ill-naturedly wounded a court official in a common street fight and was imprisoned without any apparent stimulation of his muse, who showed up later to assist the composition of canto after canto of *The Lusiads*.

Christopher Marlowe was certainly a lowlife, probably a spy as well, and was murdered in a barroom brawl. Francisco Gómez de Quevedo y Villegas (may his name lengthen like Pinocchio's nose) was repelled by the corruption he encountered at the court of Philip III, and began to scour the courtiers with satirical verses. However, having killed a negligent opponent in a duel, he ran away to Italy. There he found employment as an agent for the Duke of Orsuna, whose own political machinations backfired, bouncing Quevedo back to Spain. His satires got him in trouble again and he was shut up in a monastery for nearly four years. Roger L'Estrange became Quevedo's English translator. Both a Royalist and a Protestant, neither side in the Civil War felt they could trust him. Nor he them. All hands were correct. Although he published innumerable libelous pamphlets himself, he was an ardent opponent of the press's freedom. L'Estrange was one of our first professional men-of-letters, and so sold his pen to whoever would pay (Dr. Johnson claimed); consequently most of what he wrote is wholly forgettable. His enemies so little esteemed L'Estrange, they thought his jailing nearly beneath their notice, though he had sat in Parliament and was eighty-two when they barely troubled themselves to put him away. So much for good character! for an honest career! let us lift a glass to blind prejudice! another to deceit! each to be preferred to piety or fidelity or a foolish reluctance to cheat. Despite his numerous failings, Sir Roger's translation is a miracle.

Baldassare Castiglione managed to represent with distinction several dukes, and served as the papal nuncio to Charles V, all the while composing the courtier's handbook. *Il libro del cortegiano* is full of advice lost on most of the louts on our present list. An exception, of course, is Sir Philip Sidney who kept his character clean by dying young, offering his canteen to a common soldier though sorely wounded himself, and by having all his works published posthumously. Thomas Shadwell made the lucky mistake of angering Dryden by trying to place his Whig on the great poet's Tory. Dryden rewarded him with immortality as the target of his satire *MacFlecknoe*. Ah, and then there is the case of Camus, and the contrary case of Carlyle, and the difficult case of Céline.

The anagrammatic Alcofrybas Nasier's first satire, *Pantagruel*, was called obscene by the authorities at the Sorbonne, as was his second, *Gargantua*, and even his third, although, possibly out of weariness, they did not badger the author about the fourth. A spurious *Fifth Book of Pantagruel* was probably faked by François Rabelais in an attempt to cash in on Nasier's success. *Madame Bovary* put Flaubert in the dock, gave him his fame, as well as initiating the dyspepsia that probably killed him. Congreve was rewarded with employment as a commissioner for licensing hackney coaches, and then re-rewarded with the office of commissioner of wines, before becoming secretary to the island of Jamaica.

Cavalcanti, a friend of Dante and a Guelph to boot, was exiled to Saranza where he died of malaria. Céline was decorated for bravery, don't forget. Sébastien-Roch Nicolas Chamfort ghost-wrote for some moderate French revolutionaries. Moderation is not a revolutionary's strong suit, and during the Terror the times turned against him. He botched his suicide and died eventually of the botch. Most of his points of view were sharp and exemplary: natural ills produce in their student a contempt for death, he said, while social ills promote a contempt for life. Wordsworth, whose opinions were warm toast beside those of Chamfort, could only manage an appointment as a tax collector. *Leaves of Grass* got Whitman fired from a similar position, although Edwin Arlington Robinson held on to his sinecure at the New York Customs House until his long poems became Book Club selections.

> Edna St. Vincent Millay
> went to Paris and tried to be gay,
> but play as she might
> the rhythms weren't right
> and a Pulitzer whisked her away.
> Wrote some poems and directed a play
> in the State she decided to stay.
> To come to no harm
> she retired to a farm,
> and with seeds in her hair
> she was happier there,
> mid the romance of new mown hay.

Religion, which did so many writers in by both bullying their bodies and browbeating their brains, served François de Chateaubriand well, giving him a soft seat next to royalty, and a lot of cushy diplomatic jobs. Initially exiled to England, he returned as the French ambassador with a lady under each tender arm like loaves of French bread. No one has ever written more wonderfully about the self. How can things like this happen, we have to ask. The handsome and noble Pico della Mirandola dutifully but dangerously compiled nine hundred theses which he proposed to defend in a public speech he planned to make in Rome. The pope, however, thought otherwise, and Pico took a vacation in Paris. André Chenier was guillotined on Robespierre's order. Georges Feydeau was left undisturbed, while Hölderlin, William Collins, August Strindberg, Torquato Tasso, John Clare, Christopher Smart, Friedrich Nietzsche, Robert Walser, and William Cowper, went mad without any political encouragement. More wives went nuts than their writer-spouses, which makes sense. Aphra Behn, like Beaumarchais, was a spy for the crown, but she received so little reward for her services she was compelled to spend some time in debtor's prison, starting to write only when released. Lord Chesterton played politics like whist. The Thomases, Wycherley and Dekker, were also done in by debt. Daniel Defoe was a bankrupt too, but it was his political pamphlet, *The Shortest Way with Dissenters*, which brought him to the pillory and put him in prison. Blondel de Nesle, by singing a song they had jointly composed, located Richard Coeur de Lion in an Austrian keep, the first step in Richard's eventual escape.

Peter Porcupine spent most of his life fighting libel suits, then was convicted of sedition and sent to prison, though this did not interrupt the production of his inflammatory pamphlets. Céline, don't forget, healed the sick, while Colette bared her breast on the stage and kissed another woman on the lips. Despite support from Wittgenstein's charitable foundation, Georg Trakl was whisked into the Austrian army and shortly thereafter committed suicide. Dostoevsky associated with the wrong socialists, a group which the czar ordered rounded up and condemned, although they were, as planned, reprieved at the last moment and posted to Siberia. Instead of being struck by a bullet, he was stricken with epilepsy.

Madame de Staël pushed Benjamin Constant into politics, a game which got him exiled to Germany where he wrote *Adolphe*, his famous novel. Tides turn, and in time he became a French deputy. Terence began life as a slave, which is political enough. Thackeray, for political reasons, resigned from the staff of *Punch*. Big deal. Although Pushkin had no definite political point of view, he was banished to the Black Sea because of his youthful verses, and hounded by the censor ever after. His needless death in a stupid duel was gossiped into a government plot, consequently Pushkin became political in his afterlife. Byron's flamboyant career was also transformed into legend, even though it was legend enough the way it was lived. His self-imposed exile increased the number of his wonderful letters, and his death from a fever in far-off Greece promoted his causes at the expense of his verse.

Clarendon had another kind of character. A monarchist, he found himself finally forced to live in France after a series of failures as Lord Chancellor, including an abortive war against the Dutch. Corneille had his ups and downs but he managed to serve in Rouen's parliament for twenty-one years while establishing classical French tragedy in the rest of the country. Both brothers Grimm were exiled because of their opposition to a coup d'état by the elector of Hanover. Fray Luis de León's translation of "The Song of Songs" into Spanish was denounced by the Inquisition, and he was imprisoned. Four years later his *traduction* was forgiven. Franz Grillparzer's melancholy disposition was not improved by Metternich's censors, who hounded him. Knut Hamsun was a quisling before Quisling came along, and remained one even after his treason had been given a name. While emperor, Marcus Aurelius persecuted Christians and waged war along most of his country's borders. He nevertheless retained his status as a stoic saint. No one needs to be told once again about Disraeli. Or of John Dos Passos, who began as a liberal and ended il-. If tuberculosis is a politically produced disease, as I suspect, depending as it does on malnutrition and indifference, then it should be noted that writers as various as John Keats, D. H. Lawrence, Katherine Mansfield, Jules Laforgue, Laurence Sterne, Robert Louis Stevenson, Thomas Wolfe, Anton Chekhov, Francis Thompson, Gustavo Bécquer, and Henry David Thoreau, died of it. Perhaps we should redeem this paragraph by mentioning Benedetto Croce, who stayed a staunch opponent of Fascism, and served in the post-World War II Italian government.

Gabriele d'Annunzio, a decorated Italian patriot, had the balls to bed the Duse, and to seize Fiume in order to prevent its accession by Yugoslavia. However, his balls betrayed his brains; he was made Prince Monte Nevoso by Mussolini, and decorated, not for bravery this time, but for his Fascist fanaticism. By the victory in Florence of the Black Guelphs, Dante (he was one of the Whites) was driven into northern Italy where he drifted uneasily about dreaming of a united nation. Nathaniel Hawthorne was rewarded for his campaign biography of Franklin Pierce by an appointment as American consul to Liverpool. The book which resulted (*Our Old Home*) wasn't very good. William Dean Howells was guilty of similar hackery on behalf of Abraham Lincoln, but fared better, getting a consulship in Venice. Beckett, Camus, and Calvino, each fought nobly in the Resistance. Pérez Galdós wrote seventy-seven novels and twenty-one plays, and should have been jailed for dumping. He served, however, as a liberal delegate to his party. Blindness, the books say, put an end to his political career. Since when has this been an effective cause?

James Hogg stayed out of it by cultivating his garden. You could say the same of Quintus Horatius Flaccus. Living on a government pension, Walter de la Mare wouldn't worry a breeze. But *helas!* not Victor Hugo whose vigorous opposition to Louis Napoleon sent him into exile in Guernsey where he waited, with the greening meadows and the cows, the advent of the Third Republic. Returning, he was elected to the Senate, missing heaven by a single vote. His signet ring said: Ego Hugo. That's nicely put. Which was what happened to Leigh Hunt—election, that is—after he was imprisoned for libeling the Prince Regent. Libel also put Zola on the run. Like so many Latin American writers—Carlos Fuentes, Pablo Neruda, Alfonso Reyes, Octavio Paz—Rubén Darío spent most of his life on the outside of his country, in distant places, playing diplomatic roles. Most of the others became exiles like Guillermo Cabrera Infante, Reinaldo Arenas, and Severo Sarduy, to mention only Cubans. However, Gavin Douglas, when kicked out of Scotland, went only as far as his favored England in order to die.

According to Augusto Roa Bastos, the entire country of Paraguay exiled itself from the rest of Latin America, by virtue of "its land-locked inaccessibility, characterized by territorial segregation, internal migration, emigration, and mass exoduses." When Roa Bastos returned to Paraguay after a thirty-five-year absence, he was shortly re-expelled from the country, and copies of the book by Jorge Canese he had come to help launch were destroyed. *Agarra los libros, que no muerden.* A member of the Communist party, César Vallejo had his Paris apartment ransacked by the police. Ordered to leave France, he took up the Loyalist cause in the Spanish Civil War with a fervor hard to match, and, having returned to the city, he begged money for the Republican side on the streets of Montparnasse.

Theodore Dreiser's first novel, *Sister Carrie*, had scarcely been re-leased before it was suppressed by its publisher, Doublecross. Publishers didn't have the same success with the rest. Dryden has had his mention, but we should not omit Pope, who proves two related points: that hateful nastiness will only add to your fame if you know how to express it properly ("Flow Wellsted, flow, like thine inspirer, beer," etc.); but also that a stupid thought will remain stupid however cleverly presented ("Whatever is, is right."). The Dumas pair had mostly monetary troubles, not affairs of state. Ibsen's exile was more up-to-date than most. Lack of funds and the determined indifference of the public kept him out-of-country for twenty-seven years. His im-pregnation of a servant girl was politically conditioned if not politically caused. Jonathan Oldstyle wrote satires on New York society, while Diedrich Knickerbocker authored a *History of New York* which had a suspiciously similar style, tone, and subject matter as Oldstyle's pieces. A few years later, Geoffrey Crayon hit it big with a volume appropriately called *The Sketch Book*. However, Washington Irving's diplomatic career was consummated under his own name.

Thomas Jefferson, Abraham Lincoln, and Teddy Roosevelt, wrote rather well. None of them now would be elected. Ulysses S. Grant is another surprise. Federico García Lorca was murdered by Falangists, and Juan Ramón Jiménez fled to Cuba, then to Puerto Rico. Flavius Josephus was born Joseph ben Matthais, which tells us a good deal about his character. The governor of Galilee, he participated in the revolt of the Jews against the Romans. However, when his stronghold was overrun, he flattered his captor, Vespasian, by forecasting that brutal man's elevation to emperor. Josephus received a pension, safety, a home in Rome, and Vespasian's name, Flavius, for his trouble. Juvenal spent his life denouncing such Romans and their American-style lives, but James Joyce's departure from Ireland was merely a matter of prolonged good taste.

William Dunbar penned poems for James IV in return for a handsome life pension. *Timor mortis conturbat me.* Jean Paul earned a Bavarian stipend and kept his nose clean. Rilke's wandering was self-imposed and nonpartisan, although he preferred castles to hotels. William Blake was too utopian to be truly engagé. Lord Dunsany spent most of his nonwriting life shooting grouse, Boers, and other game, but was otherwise, like most soldiers, unpolitical. On the other hand, Rimbaud ran guns and probably traded in slaves. To the degree religious revivals are political, Jonathan Edwards was a smoking pistol, describing, in *Sinners in the Hands of an Angry God*, how things would really be if the unjust were to get their just deserts. Nikos Kazantzakis studied philosophy under Henri Bergson but turned out all right anyway, doing much left-wing work and serving as the director of the Greek Ministry of Public Welfare. Occasionally the cloth redeems itself from the smirch of divinity. Charles Kingsley, for instance, took orders, but also founded the Christian Socialist movement. His attacks on Roman Catholicism provoked Cardinal Newman's justly famous response, *Apologia pro Vita Sua*, although Kingsley can't take all the credit. Kingsley was nearly alone among the clergy in accepting Darwin's theory of evolution. Whittier wrote homespun, country-cousin verse, but earned many merit badges as an ardent abolitionist. Kipling wrote like a god and thought like the devil.

Let us move on to Kleist, another nationalist. Napoleon's troops arrested him in Berlin as a spy and deported him to France for a year. When his politically inspired newspaper failed, he and a lady friend killed themselves on the romantic shores of the Wannsee. T. S. Eliot's politics, unlike Wyndham Lewis's or Ezra Pound's, was everywhere, yet remote, like a distant smell or a sound of surf. Fontenelle's, however, was near at hand and loud, though mostly theoretical. He opposed authoritarianism, superstition, and myth, while upholding science, sense, and reason. To tote him up: he was a model man and *philosophe*. The Dreyfus case made Anatole France angry, as it should have, and his prose grew a few teeth in response. He began as a narrow partisan, attacking the church, the army, and society, but later broadened the scope of his enemies to include Man. Ben Franklin invented stoves, advised youths, drafted and signed the Declaration, spent a good part of his life in England and France where he was minister to various love affairs. Admirable man and model Philistine.

Ronsard was the court poet of Charles IX and a diplomat. He spent as much of his time in polemics as he did in poetry, but it is not clear, as it is not clear in so many other cases, whether the distractions which made up daily life and political duty actually deprived us of anything he might have written in their stead. La Bruyère could not have been more political, if we consider the cast and content of his work, which aphoristically exposed the cupidity, stupidity, hypocrisy, arrogance, and indolence of the upper classes. His only real punishment for this effrontery seems to have been a delay in his election to the French Academy. Philip Freneau, whose family was French Huguenot, was a sailor. Captured by the English, he wrote *The British Prison Ship* in revenge and restitution, and, in consequence, became known as the Poet of the Revolution. Choderlos de Laclos was arrested during the Terror, and fled the country for a time. Back in Paris, he was detained again, but under Napoleon he became a general, and died at Taranto, although his perspicacious cynicism seems to have predeceased him.

Both *Emile* and *The Social Contract* were censored by the authorities, and Rousseau felt compelled to live abroad in consequence. He believed that God, Man, and Nature—each and all—were good. Somehow only society, with its penchant for private property and its encouragement of unnatural desires, was evil. Unfortunately, history, even in his own time, had already shown that God did not exist, Nature was indifferent, and Man was a murderous thug. Nevertheless, Rousseau is still read. There is always an accounting for bad taste. Ruskin, on our happier hand, is rarely read. Perhaps this is because he became a social reformer, and therefore a bore, with his later work, when he wrote imaginary letters to artisans and common laborers advising them to unionize, establish a pension plan, and support a form of national education. Excellence is not always interesting. Bertrand Russell split his intellectual energies between logic, mathematics, epistemology, and a pacifist humanitarian social agenda—efforts for which he received misunderstanding, disbelief, or calumny. He died (only to write its name) at Penrhyndeudraeth.

Théophile Gautier neither gave nor received trouble from the state. He is on this meandering riverlike list because, in my opinion, the modern literary movement began with his attack upon the philistinism of the bourgeois in his famous preface to *Mademoiselle de Maupin* (1835). It was in "the age of cotton nightcaps," as Albert Guérard so aptly calls it, that Gautier, peeved to the point of plain speech, wrote: "There is nothing truly beautiful but that which can never be of any use whatever; everything useful is ugly, for it is the expression of some need, and man's needs are ignoble and disgusting like his own poor and infirm nature. The most useful place in a house is the water-closet."

Once upon a time, writers received their principal patronage from the church, and were often clerics of some kind themselves. Otherwise writers were attached to lowly feudal dukes, landlocked barons, or illiterate earls. They were secretaries, spies, diplomats, preachers, advisers, soldiers, politicians. Gibbon, for instance, was a captain in the grenadiers, but he was a member of Parliament by the time the first volumes of his *History* began to appear. Had he written his chapters on the history of Christianity a century before, he would surely have been incarcerated, and incinerated almost any time earlier. As it was, he only suffered notoriety, as David Hume would later.

The case of Thomas Sackville is exemplary. He was born to a well-placed family, and was able to enter Parliament at the age of twenty-two. He found favor (as they used to say) with Queen Elizabeth who made him a baron. With a friend, Thomas Norton, he wrote what is often called the first Elizabethan tragedy, *Gorboduc*. He took over the editorship of a verse series, *A Mirror for Magistrates*, to which he contributed some important lyrics. His public career was distinguished to a fault: he was, in turn, an English emissary to other nations, a member of the Privy Council and a Knight of the Garter, Oxford's chancellor, and eventually Lord Treasurer of the Realm. He died in harness, as the Earl of Dorset, at a council meeting in Whitehall. A career of this kind is, for a writer in any industrially advanced Western nation, nearly inconceivable now.

Dropouts became country curates. They didn't commit crimes, either of person or poetry. They lived quietly, spoke softly, and specialized in rural themes. A few clerked or held small odd jobs. It did not do, like Burns, to be frolicsome. But most writers didn't choose writing as their profession. Writing was a hobby, undertaken as proof of one's breeding, sensitivity, and breadth, or because one felt the need to reflect on life as it had been led. Rarely did it turn into a career. And their attitude toward society was not determined by the fact that they believed themselves to be "artists." Nor was their experience of men, women, and the world postponed until they had received an advanced degree and gotten their first job. Gradually, the clergy's hold on the culture weakened, to be replaced by the overtly political—that is to say, by the new Nation-State.

By the middle of the nineteenth century, however, when Sainte-Beuve was pursuing his career, bright young men were starting life at a later age, studying medicine or the law, and might—but only if they strayed from the course their family had appointed for them—consider writing their vocation. Nevertheless, such a choice not only meant one would probably end up a journalist, but suffer a concomitant fall in social estimation. Sainte-Beuve was exceptionally successful: he fell in with Hugo's crowd, published a scandalous novel, wrote an influential weekly newspaper column, became a powerful arbiter of public taste, and ended in the Senate.

When writing was a marginal activity of mainstream men, writing was the major medium of communication, and you could be punished for annoying the people in power; but when writing became the principal concern of marginal figures, it ceased to have the significance it once had. The more important the word, the more important the writer. Greek culture, being essentially oral, gave the word every weight, but the word was also as evanescent as an odor, and had to be sensed, savored, saved, set down in the mind; for which reason poetry, oratory, and even argument, emphasized sound, meter, symmetry, and peppered its passages with epithets and formulas. Writing gave the word permanence. What you said could not outlast living memory, but what you wrote could be held against you by generations yet to draw their genes. Printing allowed the word a width the word had never had. Nevertheless, the more words there were, the less value was given to any one of them. The word was worth most when it was incised on a tablet of clay; it was worth least when it announced bargains on a newspaper insert, through a radio ad, or in a throwaway.

The connection between speaking and being for Socrates could not be closer or more complete, and even for orators like Cicero and Quintilian, the breech between speech and business was thin as a sibilant. With writing the word became a means, and its essence was soon separate from the sense it bore, and it fell into the callous hands of paraphrase. As eloquence declined, men possessed a poorer posture, became less elegant of voice and complex of character, while nature became a yawning bore. Nowadays, a belief in the power of the literary word is confined to backward countries and is a leading indicator of a less advanced society.

Latin American authors, as we have seen, are not strangers to diplomacy (and the citizens of their country honor them, listen to them, even pay them heed), even though the most notable live cautiously abroad. Soviet writers have also had huge and eager audiences, even when what they were eager for was rarely received. In Africa, too, liberation has so often been the door to tyranny, and the historical importance of the bard meant he would soon bear scars upon his back. A few avoided harm by escaping to the top, like heat up a flue. Léopold Sédar Senghor, for instance, labored for his country's freedom for twelve years, and when it was finally realized, he became president of the Senegalese Republic. Similarly, Agostinho Neto played the partisan's role. In the same year in which Senegal achieved its independence, Neto became the head of a movement for the liberation of Angola. He was almost immediately arrested, escaping confinement after two years in a Lisbon jail. Eventually he too would occupy a presidential chair. Ezekiel Mphahlele, forbidden to teach in his native South Africa, was forced into exile in Nigeria. He did not return to South Africa for twenty years. Likewise Alex La Guma and Dennis Brutus have seen the intestinal interiors of South African jails. Even in Senghor's Senegal, Sembène Ousmane's scripts and films have been torn by the censor's teeth. After his confinement during the Nigerian Civil War, Wole Soyinka, like so many other African writers, chose exile in France before returning, after a lapse of years, to the country of his birth. Kofi Awoonor came back to Ghana after a distinguished career at State University of New York, Stony Brook, only to be imprisoned a year for his alleged connection with an abortive coup. The authorities in Kenya did not trouble to try Ngũgĩ wa Thiong'o. They merely put him away for a while to protect the public's ears from the harshly unpleasant sound of the truthful word.

In every country, in every clime, for any color, at any time, orthodoxy acts evilly toward its enemies. Survival is its single aim: that is, to rigidify thought, sterilize doubt, cauterize criticism, mobilize the many to brutalize the few who dare to dream beyond the borders of their village, the walls of their room, the conventions of their community, the givens of some God, the smother of custom, or the regimen of an outmoded morality; and even the Greatest Good itself could not fail to be bruised by such handling, and rapidly rot where the bruise had been. One sign of a sound idea is its fearlessness. Protect the truth and you put it away in the same place you have put those enemies you have saved it from. And any time a zealot speaks against freedom on behalf of a sacred thought, we must always listen for the anxiety in the voice, for such a voice is worried only about itself: to protect the profits it presently enjoys, to prevent the losses it fears in the future, and to avoid the penalties which just such fanatics have paid in the past for their presumption.

Wang Meng can look back on a life of both servility and service, with his unpretentious short stories causing consternations at twenty-year intervals. In 1956, he published "The Young Newcomer in the Organization Department"—a scathing picture of bureaucratic inertia that started a firestorm in the dry forest of officials. Wang Meng was pronounced a "rightist" and the Cultural Revolution swept him away to do menial work at Ili in Xinjiang. In 1976, he was repatriated and made a party member again. He immediately demonstrated his resiliency by writing "The Butterfly"—the ironic tale of a time-serving bureaucrat who falls afoul of the Young Turks in charge of purification, and is publicly humiliated by his own son who boxes his ears and jeers as his father is banished to Mongolia. Yet in that barren backward place, the bureaucrat finds some meaning, a little love, and brief happiness, only, when abruptly restored to office, to return, unimproved, to his feebly inefficient and pampered ways. Widely admired for the staunchness of his character as well as the fearless honesty of his work, Wang Meng was made the minister of culture, only to be forced from his position by the Party after the Tian'anmen catastrophe.

André Gide's defense of homosexuality (*Corydon*) created such a scandal, he sold his property and went to Africa. There, and now politically alert, he was witness to the abuses of colonialism. Still politically alert, he was not taken in by the façades of fraternity and freedom erected around the USSR by its sycophants, or by its propaganda promises either, and was roundly criticized by the Left for not sharing its inexcusably self-serving trust in what was always a dubious ideal. Gide sneaked back to France but only so far as Cannes. And kept his mouth shut.

The forces arrayed against the writer have so far been—in the order of their periods of domination—the Tribe, the Church, the Nation-State, Society at Large or what is called Public Opinion, and the quieter, politer, more effective pressures of the marketplace, the so-called Commercial and Consumer World. The influence of the first is based upon accidents of birth, blood, and color; that of the second on ignorance and fear expressed in superstitions; that of the third on power, punishments, and prison; that of the fourth on gossip, bigotry, pettiness, and parochialism; while that of the last is built on our faith in money, on "mememoreme" (in Joyce's coinage), and on the inexhaustible gullibility of greed. Now that all these fighters are noisily in the field, each contestant always endeavors to enlist (or, if not, discount) the influence and support of the others. In the first instance, personal identity is a matter of family and race: we have the same nose length, hair kink, language habits, food fads, festivals, heroes, history, hates (I am a Serb); in the second, your creed counts: types of taboo, principal heresies, hierarchies, holy days and sacred relics, rationales, rites and routines, saints, symbols, and monetary contributions (I am a Sufi); in the third, patriotism with its slogans and its flags, describes you: which includes all the grain which waves, the armies which bear the country's banner into battle—bless our boys!—the long and distinguished Past which chauvinism always creates to glorify the Nation (despite all the bad luck and betrayal it has suffered), yes, San Juan Hill defines you, Remember the Maine! and the Marine Hymn defines you too, somewhat the way you are defined by your town's baseball team (I am a Chicago Cubbie); in the fourth, common concerns and the character of daily lives, inherited values, shared myths, convenient scapegoats, and conspiracies of blindness— a kind of stew made of the leftovers from the other four—do the literal trick (I am a Southerner); while, lastly, the self is seen as a rack of clothes, as an address and a set of wheels, a position in the bank, a diet designed for our modern life, as a lot of fun-filled leisure activities, as a suitable set of sexual practices selected from technicolor picture books (I am a Playboy or his pliant and pettable Bunny), each sale item understood to be a part of an installment lifestyle, naturally subject to change—to cite an instance, when I trade in my former personality for a later model, one with more options, more efficiency, more allure, more speed.

Jean Giraudoux served prewar France in the Ministry of Foreign Affairs, and during World War I was a soldier; then he spent World War II as the director of information for the French Republic, and finally worked for the Vichy government in the same capacity, slipping from one regime to another like the eloquent eel he was. George Gissing's subject was poverty, which he knew first hand. You can write about poverty without being political, and a great many have, because poverty is fun to read about—full of human sentiments and local color. However, Gissing dealt with the *effects* of poverty, and no one cares to read about that—sordid stuff best left hidden behind the silence of neglect. People like Pater, Patmore, and Peacock did not drink from the bubbler of politics, whereas Peele (for we are somewhere in the Ps by now) appears to have abstained only from the vote, dying of drunkenness and syphilis so obscurely the date of his death is a "circa." Dylan Thomas was also no slouch as a souse.

Killed or wounded in a war: Rupert Brooke, Wilfred Owen, Siegfried Sassoon, Charles Péguy, probably Ambrose Bierce, then Edward Thomas, Isaac Rosenberg, Henri Alain-Fournier, Guillaume Apollinaire—just a few from a long long list. Suicides: Sergei Yesenin, who wrote his last poem with blood from his slit wrist before hanging himself; Walter Benjamin, who lost all hope of escaping the Nazis; Paul Celan and Primo Levi who postponed their deaths in the camps

William H. Gass

until later on in so-called "liberated" life; Gérard de Nerval, who hung himself from a sewer grate by an apron string which he had bragged to his friends had been Mme de Maintenon's belt or was the garter of Marguerite de Valois; Hart Crane, who jumped from the stern of a ship, perhaps in despairing memory of the sailors who had beaten up and pleasured him; Chatterton, who could not have guessed that the manner of his death would make his literary career last a little longer than his life had; Virginia Woolf, pockets filled with stones to drag her body under where her spirit was; José Silva, whose manuscript was shipwrecked; Cesare Pavese, Communist in spite of himself, unable to commit to a world so woeful; Mayakovsky, the Soviet's first "Poet Laureate," who once wrote, in his poem to Pushkin, "I am now free from love and from posters," although, unfortunately, he was free of neither, writing poetry with one hand and propaganda with the other, and shooting himself in the heart when he should have shot himself through the poster.

Alfred de Vigny's play *Chatterton*, expressed the nineteenth-century writer's disillusionment with society and the values that gave it suck. His hardheaded rejection of political and religious solutions to Europe's problems, unfortunately involved a sentimentalizing of the remote poet, the disinterested philosopher, the objective scientist. It may indeed be necessary to cleanse one's ideals of political and religious taints, and preserve them in a protective solitude; however, if so distantly removed, they will only shine in emptiness, and no one shall see any better because of their light.

Lord Acton knew of the evils he warned his students about through his years of close acquaintance with the monied, privileged, and powerful. Although he never published his lectures during his lifetime, there are many posthumous collections. The correct version of his famous and frequently misquoted axiom is: "Power tends to corrupt; absolute power corrupts absolutely." Has anyone composed an aphorism about what damage impotence does? or how good corruption feels? Are we to believe that passivity promotes virtue? Georg Büchner organized a revolutionary secret society, and issued a fiery pamphlet called *The Hessian Courier*, which got its message under way with the following wonderful sentence: "The life of the Aristocrats is a long Sunday: they live in beautiful houses, they wear elegant clothes, they have fat faces, and they speak a language of their own;

whereas the people lie at their feet like manure on the fields." He was forced to vacate his native haunts, and fled to Zurich, but contracted typhus there and died at the age of twenty-three without having seen a line of his three plays performed.

Prison is a productive place to put writers. Think of all the famous books that have been penned there, all the executions that have hastened undying lines into existence. But the jailers have few reasons to rejoice, for it is in their jails that men, who had formerly no thought or sentiment to put on paper that could not be framed in dulcet words of love, have composed their most politically inflammatory works. *Mein Kampf* for instance. Nor, as this little run through history shows, have all of the jailed been jugged for writing reasons. Some were crooks, some spies, some were thought to be dangerous on other grounds, some backed the wrong pretender, some connived to the point of treason, a few were simply unlucky in their friends, or were caught in catastrophes too general to be choosy about who was carried down. And occasionally a government (even one of those) will feel sorry for some noxious fly in its ointment, and pension the rascal, as the British crown did William Godwin, in the twilight of his life and in the shadow of his bankruptcy. Godwin's feminist wife Mary Wollstonecraft died shortly after the birth of her first legitimate child, punished for her indelicate life and liberal leanings by Motherhood, society's heaviest club against women.

Consider the case of Matthew Prior whose first writings were burlesques. His career as a diplomat was long and distinguished: a secretary to the English ambassador at The Hague, an aide at the negotiations for the Treaty of Ryswick, a member of Parliament, and a principal participant in framing the Treaty of Utrecht, called, on account of his role in it, "Matt's Peace." When Queen Anne, his protectress, died, he was put under house arrest, and in such restricted circumstances Prior returned to the writing of poetry, composing two long works that are today mostly forgotten, while the little scraps of lyric verse he jotted down in spare moments during his years at court and conference table are deliciously alive. Prison may prime the pen, but the sincerity of the writer's surroundings do not ensure success. Swift was another who had to leave England with the passing of Queen Anne and the fall of her party. Like many serious satirists, he was a Tory. He took no chances with *Gulliver's Travels*, which, he said, was written to "vex the world rather than divert it," and published it anonymously.

In men, talent and character are rarely in balance. Too often, one trait is weak where the other is strong, and weakness (whose awesome power makes its name a misnomer) wrestles with strength (whose deplorable flaws make its fall, like Samson's, as simple as a snip, as sure as death) and pins it to some pusillanimous page. Weakness, like a steady drip, wears confidence and skill and talent down though each be sturdy as a stone. When Gogol, a case in point, died, he owned only some old clothes (an overcoat, surely) and a couple of hundred books; so Moscow University underwrote his funeral, a rite which did more damage to the state than his work. Admirers, passing his bier, pulled dead flowers from the dead man's hands, and the czar felt so threatened by the widespread display of grief he kept any notice of Gogol's burial from appearing in the press. Turgenev was arrested for writing the obit.

In the same vein, the many minor virtues that Tocqueville discovered in America could not make up for its major flaw: an inherently low level of creativity; and only in those cases where the writer is so gifted he can be a wastrel with his reason and pontificate to his heart's content as Tolstoy did, or damage his prose without doing it utterly in, as Faulkner was inclined to (believing that a thinker won his Prize and not a word-drunk chronicler), can catastrophe be escaped; or a woman may run the risk of remaining both woman and writer, if she is sufficiently resolute about her work as to overcome the need to certify herself by having children instead of books; for how many children had Lady Colette, or Stein, or Cather, or Eliot, or Woolf, or Porter, or Jewett, or Dickinson, or Bishop, or Moore, or Gabriela Mistral, or Flannery O'Connor? George Sand bore two before leaving them and her husband for freedom. Madame de Staël began by having affairs instead of kids, but then, in exile from the Terror, had two with her nobleman lover. However, she could turn their care over to her not inconsiderable household staff. Back in Paris she became the mistress of Benjamin Constant, but both were banished by Napoleon to her family estate on the shores of Lake Geneva. She certainly could never have been called Madame Constant, and eventually this husband was replaced by a strapping young soldier, as Madame usurped still another prerogative of the male. Benjamin consoled himself with a second wife (the first one he abandoned for de Staël) and continued that successful political career I spoke of earlier. However, the emperor he served remained of the dominant sex, and that emperor (once made sour, never to be sweetened) kept de Staël and her books out of France until he was forced from the throne and into exile himself.

If Godwin was given a pension when the government heard the reassuring rattle of his death and realized that retirement payments would not be perpetual, Carlo Goldoni lost his when the Terror took such support away from all the greencarders who had served the monarchy (Goldoni taught Italian to several Bourbon princesses). Thus rewarded, he died in Parisian poverty. On the other hand, a poet like Petrarch always had patrons, and sailed over perilous political waters as if he were a sea bird, not a ship. Patronage has always been a vexing problem, because patrons of the arts, whether private, or public like our National Endowment for the Arts, rarely realize that what they are supporting are the general possibilities of production in an artist's life, with its shifts of direction and qualitative ups and downs, not specific works with certifiable standards or previously approved points of view. That is, what is being encouraged is a certain kind of climate, not rain on a specific day.

Still, prison is an appropriate place to put authors. It gives them a sense of grievance, and we know that grievances are among a writer's more powerful motives; it removes them from temptations, and we know how easily writers are tempted by bosom or by bottle to imbibe; it eliminates distractions, that of the housewife among the more miserable, and makes pointless all the petty steps that must be taken in order to advance one's commercial, scholarly, or political career; it directs the mind to the main things: liberty, injustice, the misery of humankind, the irremediable loss of opportunity, man's vast immemorial waste of Time, now seen as not some abstract flow of tick to tock, but as the lit wick of life itself blown out, and the dead candle's thin timorous thread of smoke still unaccountably mistaken for the flame.

Pierre Joseph Proudhon—now there is a name to remember with amusement—certainly occupies a place of distinction in Albert Guérard's gallery of Philistines, along with Victor Hugo, Voltaire, and Ben Franklin (my nomination for the finest exemplar of the form). I should also like to recommend H. G. Wells, a splendid specimen. But Proudhon had as vapid a mind as has latterly been invented, and his inept poaching on revolutionary ground (he was prosecuted often and imprisoned on at least one occasion) drove Karl Marx to answer Proudhon's *The Philosophy of Misery* with a turnaround of his own, *The Misery of Philosophy.* Isaac Babel wasn't simply picked on either. He served in the czar's army, then in the revolutionary forces, and finally in the secret police. Or were these falsehoods placed upon the record by the Stalinist wretches who purged him? (Danilo Kiš has written wonderfully about this sort of "documentary identity.") In any case, relatives and friends began immediately to erase the erroneous data, and to add their own air to an already clouded issue. He worked on a stud farm—yes or no? What counts, of course, is the reality of the evil tide that swept such a writer away. It was Proudhon who said, "Property is theft." Under Stalin, the person of the writer became the property of the state.

Putting writers in prison is preferable to putting them upon a pedestal. Giving an author influence is like giving him poison. His pen begins to froth at the nib. He not only continues to manufacture baloney, he begins to eat it himself. Soon, like Faulkner and Tolstoy, he is a victim of runaway megalomania. Alexander Solzhenitsyn's opinions are those of someone still in the pay of a dead czar.

Of course, when state oppression has reached its highest level of efficiency, walls will no longer be necessary; fear will put bars on every window, as Miklós Haraszti has so sardonically described in his analysis of its action in *The Velvet Prison.*

No, I say. Put 'em in the cold stone pokey. Make their suffering visible to themselves. They will be better for it. They will overcome adversity and triumph in the end. Censorship simply makes writers devious; it gives them a sense of importance; without oppression— without poverty and unhappiness—they would have nothing to write about, nothing to complain of, nothing to demand be changed. We wouldn't have *The Enormous Room* if the French military hadn't jailed e. e. cummings by mistake for three months. Thomas Nashe was confined for his contribution to *The Isle of Dogs*, so that overly authored, weakly comic play cannot be called a gaol's consequence but a jail's cause. Wilde's poem is quite another matter of course. Jean Giono's sojourn in prison for pacifism seems not to have had any loud literary upshot; whereas Irina Ratushinskaya wrote poetry before, during, and after the KGB sent her into internal exile. That suffering ennobles, that oppression improves, is an old canard. Let us not worry about the evil effects of too much happiness. Happiness is not a habit of the human race. Misfortune is its forte.

We do not remember these writers for their political accomplishments, even if the Treaty of Utrecht was, for a time, called "Matt's Peace." The poet/politician produces two sorts of worldly effects: the document he signs, the plots for whose unmasking he plays the snitch, the preferments his flattery of the powerful obtains, the sagacious point of view his experience provides, the lessons his pupils learn (John Skelton was tutor to Henry VIII), the speeches he puts in the mouth of a monarch who otherwise would only mumble; that bunch of business on the one hand, while on the other there are the verses he indites, the plays he puts upon the stage, the lines that linger in the memory, thoughts that are carried by their ingenious rhymes into other countries and to other times; and, as the System sees it, that's the danger, for a sword thrust in some real Polonius's side brings out only the poor man's blood, while the stage's imagined figure becomes proverbial, the meaning of his merely simulated death deep; because the reality of the work of art is what terrifies the tyrant who has so much terror of his own to spread; yet all of his effects are linear and begin to weaken the moment they exist; whereas the merest phrase, turned on the tongue as though it were a lathe, outlasts and reappears, and is remembered—not Agincourt and what the English arrows did upon that field, but Shakespeare's speech in praise of Crispin's Day.

Words are persuasions poured into the ear, revelations delivered to the reading eye. Simple syllables speak the deed that won't wash off. So, ironically, it is the Ruler, his Law, and its Officials who have thrown some wretch for theft or debt or slander into their keeps, where they ignore their prisoner as if the world were asleep; and then lend paper, put pen in his feeble hand, before unwittingly releasing him later, only subsequently to read of what their reign, their command of the country, has come to—who have made possible the very text that they condemn, and ban, and rail against, and confiscate; since it is by means of such sequestered works that both they and the world learn what has been done, not just to one brief thief or pitiful pauper, but, through social inequity, corrupt officials, steep taxes, adventurous policies (I keep the list brief), how a people have been oppressed, and what their rule has meant to an entire, now bankrupt, nation.

Then, awake at last . . . the authorities . . . hurt, smarting from the imagined injustice of it (since authorities never see themselves as evil) . . . the authorities . . . a victim of exaggeration surely, yet fearful of these lies and their spread . . . the authorities . . . with futile efficiency, act to halt the beat of the angry heart their beloved prison patterned, now much too late, well after the rhythms of the poet's lines have made their music sound in the souls of the king's subjects (or perhaps they're called the Commonwealth's Citizens, Color's Brothers, or just Comrades of the Cause, anyone over whom the authorities presume to have authority), and with that misleading rhetoric, those false reports, much innuendo, their raucous sounds, have not only turned Brotherhood's Beleaguered Legions round to lean against that Crown, so the people now refuse the colored shirt that's offered them, the mock military cap, won't wave symbol-bearing flags, or wear any armband other than one of mourning; but listen instead to the rhythms, stanzas, music, the significant sounds, which are freeing them to feel the outrage, the courage, the verses contain, or the passion the prose holds, where resolution and disdain, or realization and rejection, live; for public power, though it can kill countless and maim more, is like water in the hand, and all its decrees are tardy; nor will the fall of the state itself raise a spiff more dust than any other violent act; the noise of it will die away; but, like the body of Orpheus, torn to pieces, the poem will still find a head to sing through, and, though the poet's remains have been flung into the river, the poem will still contrive a way to float its song above the water; that is what galls the tyrant, stops every blue nose's nostrils with snot his snorting can never clear, and drives them to their excesses: what does the sword say? the sword says swat! take that! bleed a lot! while the pen says—simply—that *it* is mightier, and proves its own point with the phrase.

That is how the myth runs, when written by the writer, of how it shall be with every society, every despot, who refuses to allow and to heed the free word.

Yet the confusions of history, which convulse every truth with the ailment of its opposite, cannot be escaped. Caprice is another king, Chance another feudal lord, Luck another castle. Irony is Sincerity's secret lover. Bruno Schultz wrote his stories and taught drawing in the boy's college at Drohobycz. It was not an easy life. His family responsibilities were heavy. Poor, he etched his drawings on spoiled photographic plates he was able to obtain from pharmacies. His work had won him prizes and some renown in Warsaw, but the drudgery of daily life had worn him down, and he had broken off a troubled engagement with a woman of another faith. First the Soviets, then the Germans, occupied his town. Fortune smiled its crooked smile. One of the Nazi officers admired his paintings, and took the Jew, Bruno Schultz, under his protective wing—the Jew, Bruno Schultz, who, from caution, had ceased writing. One morning, Schultz was fetching home a loaf of bread when he was shot in the open street by a Gestapo agent who had a grudge against his "patron." The cemetery Bruno Schultz was buried in has, itself, been liquidated. No account I've seen tells us where the bread fell when Bruno Schultz did. Clearly, the only writer present was the one killed.

The superiority of the word to the deed, which I've alleged, does not mean the word redeems the deed. The word redeems nothing, for nothing is redeemable. Is death to be praised for all the poems it has inspired denouncing it? When the *Deutschland* sank on its way to England, many drowned, among them five Franciscan nuns. Sad as the news was, as numerous the loss, it was the death of those nuns that provoked the imagination of Gerard Manley Hopkins. A priest, he had to ask permission to write a poem on the subject. This poem appears to have released his dark, nearly demented muse, to give us his major poems. Should nuns be ticketed on every overloaded ferry, now, just in case?

Bertolt Brecht said he changed his country more often than his shoes, and demonstrated how unstable the real artist is, if you wish to build a political position on his ground; for his plays adhered too ardently to the particular to be trusted to support a slogan, and saw too far, and felt too much, to be satisfactory guides for action. His own Galileo puts it properly: "You have two rival spirits lodged inside you. You have got to have the pair. Stay disputed, undecided. Stay a whole, stay divided. Embrace the crude one, praise the pure. Be clean. Be obscene. Keep them bedded." Brecht spent World War II in Los Angeles, where his rented bungalow is on the expatriate German culture tour (Schönberg, the Manns, Adorno, and others). Your tour guide will also point out the house nearby that the FBI used to spy on him.

Our writers have been of every persuasion. Some have been foolish, others bright, a few upright, most rather average in that line, many mean and suspicious, a lot disloyal, unscrupulously ambitious, carpy, dishonest, hell-bent and promiscuous. Neither the High-Minded, nor the High-Handed, neither Low-Lifes nor Low-Brows, Well-Born nor Ne'r-Do-Wells, the widely traveled nor the narrowly circumscribed, the broadly educated nor the specialized, are privileged to the literary life; and their various modes of existence are in no case safe indicators of the aesthetic qualities of such texts as they may author. Remember, for instance, that Edmund Spenser supported England's oppressive policies in Ireland, where he lived most of his life until the Irish burned his Kilcolman castle in the Civil War. No, there isn't a single important point of view that has not been beautifully praised. There is scarcely an important truth that hasn't been brilliantly traduced. Sigh as one must at the medieval escapism of William Morris, but don't let that color your appreciation of the common sense and sturdy prose of *News from Nowhere*. Despise mysticism as a positivist ought, but not the poems of St. John of the Cross, who, as a Carmelite reformer, was kidnapped and imprisoned by members of his own sect. Doubt the truth of the pope's church from catacomb to spire, but do not doubt the honor of Robert Southwell, who was arrested while celebrating mass, wrestled to the Tower and put upon the rack, where he refused to reveal the names of his fellow priests, though he lost his life at Tyburn for it; nor fail, either, to admire the beauty of his verse. The career of Sir Thomas More needs no recital. Politics, Moral Fiber, and Art may intertwine, but there is an essential difference between one vine and the other.

But this is not the popular opinion. George Meredith's first novel, *The Ordeal of Richard Feverel*, was withdrawn by its publishers as immoral. "O what a dusty answer gets the soul," he wrote, "when hot for certainties in this our life." Molière was hounded his entire career by religious zealots. Calderón de la Barca, on the other hand, began work as a playwright at the court of Philip IV and ended it writing *autos sacramentales*. Lope de Vega's problems were mainly personal. He was banished from Madrid for libeling his mistress. Nor did taking holy orders slow him down. It's estimated now that he wrote fifteen hundred plays—many more than his mostly unfortunate affairs. Around men, women died in their birthing beds. Copulation enslaves but breeding kills. Karl Kraus, the pacifist and Viennese Cassandra, was listened to, for he repeated the words of the politicians in the pages of *Die Fackel* and on the stage before thousands of entertained ears, reading the papers the way New York's Mayor La Guardia read the funnies, allowing everyone to see and smell the shit that came out of their leaders' mouths. Yet there was never enough irony, never enough outrage. Wars make wonderful battlefields, Kraus suggested, and battlefields are pleasant places to picnic. They listened. They laughed. They applauded. But they didn't change their ways. Thomas Bernhard castigated similar crowds, with the same result.

It may be difficult to admire the bourgeois sensibility behind Isaac Bickerstaff's *Tatler*, but if you wish to read a fine work rich in political observation, the recommendation here is Montesquieu's *Persian Letters*.

Hush, little baby, don't say a word, mama's going to buy you a mockingbird. Don't say this word; don't say that one; you might give offense; you might uncover to others a squalid condition, even of your own; you might affront, disturb, step on a toe, put a nose out of joint. In the same moment a word is banned, a thought denied utterance, a point of view shut down for the season, the writer has a holy obligation to search for a sentence that will contain it, seek a place to speak the thought raucously aloud, formulate the point of view, not as if it were his own, but as eloquently as if it were his own.

What is unthinkable? Think it. What is unutterable? Utter it. What cannot be spelled without a dash? Fill in the dashes with doubts. What is obscene? Dream it. In all its tones, in seamy detail, at indelicate length. What is too horrible to contemplate? Describe it. With cool and indifferent interest. As though peeling a peach. You will not be the first, for the unthinkable has already been thought, the unutterable uttered innumerable times, God's various names have been taken in vain, the obscene enjoyed, the horrible carried out. This is the value of Miller, Genet, Burroughs, Sade, and Céline. Even the simplest thought, given the simplest form, must be uttered as though cast into a context that contains all of its conceivable opposites—not so that it will waffle, but so it will be strong. But that means, for all those who lack confidence in the resilience of their ideas, that every fine line, even if it seems to be standing securely on your side, is open in its confident stride to every other pace, realizes the great range of human attitude and feeling on every issue, and invites these differences along; and what narrow mind or intolerant ear or suspicious eye wants that kind of crowd?

Writers constantly complain that political institutions fail, in the end, to improve mankind, but encourage it in its foolhardy rush to the abyss, and if there's any hesitation at the brink, to give the mugwump a hefty push. Rarely has contempt been so thoroughly earned as Man's for Man. Karl Kraus who in 1914, spoke sardonically of living "*in dieser grossen Zeit*" said: "Mankind consists of customers. Behind flags and flames, heroes and helpers, behind all fatherlands an altar has been erected at which pious science wrings its hands: God created the consumer! Yet God did not create the consumer that he might prosper on earth but for something higher: that the dealer might prosper on earth, for the consumer was created naked and becomes a dealer only when he sells clothes." So all those guys who dealt Adam his first pair of pants (fuckfellows, now, with the politicos), in order to make one final sale, offer to us souvenirs of the last day, naturally in advance of the event.

In all fairness, though, shouldn't we ask how far up the slope of Mt. Perfection our literature has helped us climb? Are we better now that Calvino has written? that Rilke has rhymed? that even as you read, on some machine, beauty is being made? and do those great lines to which, a few pages previously, I made my bow, and praised for their power, their memorable nature, and their superiority to simple history . . . do they succeed in lessening our greediness, moderating our passions, and rendering less dull our sensitivity to suffering? Isn't there enough pain behind all our calluses already? when there's no longer anywhere to look away to, as some once looked away to Dixieland—no place to gaze without its being on grief?

I am asking for a list of great good things that we can tell the world were accomplished because Menander wrote a play, or Goethe made us weep at Werther's fate. Was I cleansed by Saint Genet? or even by my hero, Karl Kraus, was I rescued from any folly? for did I not do lunch one day at the peak of Pickett's charge? and look up from Jane Austen to bitch at my children? or yell "that-a-way" at a headline when we beat up on Iraq? and nod like a sage when I read

what Pavese—another fallen hero—wrote: "One nail drives out another. But four nails make a cross." One nod signifies agreement, two
nods sleep. So can't we say to Mrs. Grundy: "Literature, lady, wets
no underpants; don't blame us for your children's iniquities."? And
can't we properly protest to the police that they are locking away innocence, for what book has brought a robber baron into being between its crafty pages? what steamy scene outheats the action in the
slowest stew? No, my lord, literature is noble, therefore it desires to
do nothing, does nothing, says nothing, is nothing, harms no one,
opens not a single eye, or puts an untoward thought in any mind;
and therefore writing should receive your scorn, perhaps, because a
waste of words is the idlest of all voids, the dullest of deserts; but,
sire, such vagrancy should not receive your prison's appointments
when there's so much genuine demand, or your censor's attention
either, when there's buggery going on in the bushes; no, let we writers write freely, prate away; we shall, if ignored, not even fright a gnat
from its spoiling orange.

Imagine Montaigne as the mayor of Bordeaux, Berkeley as a bishop,
Richard Brinsley Sheridan as secretary to the Treasury, Sophocles a general, Yeats a senator, Mallarmé a school teacher, Voltaire amassing a fortune through a series of shrewd investments, O'Casey as a labor leader,
Wallace Stevens behind an insurance adjuster's desk, Trollope as a postal
inspector, Samuel Clemens, steamboat pilot, Disraeli, prime minister,
Paul Valéry, for twenty-two years a private secretary to the director of
a news agency; and then imagine any contemporary writer in a similar
position: what serious artist would now ally himself with the incarnation
of Mammon, big business? what writer not simply wanting to promote
himself would run for an important public office? or work, even for
a time as West and Faulkner did, in Hollywood? or ever have the dubious opportunity to order soldiers "over the top"? What writing
woman, perhaps as femme fatale, would enlist in the CIA? or would
be allowed to take a turn as Emma Goldman or even run another
Hull House? A lonely priest, perhaps, is still possible, a convict is more
than likely, a whore, somebody deep in shopfront social work, an oc-
casional physician or lawyer, contemplating retirement, a guy running
a gay gym, but a movie actor? a baseball player? a pipefitter? a banker?
That's why the recent election of Vaclav Havel, the candidacy of
Mario Vargas Llosa, and the transnational threats to Salman Rushdie
seem so ahistorical and horrific, and require our reconsideration of

the entire relation between these two, far different, much impinging, realms. Because normally we teach; we serve as publisher's scouts; we edit a little; we hire out; we teach; we don't dabble any more in diplomacy; we don't hold office, only office hours; we occasionally cover the news; we teach; now and then we still inherit, otherwise we teach; we run a dusty bookstore, drop out, push a private press; we teach; very occasionally we hit it big with a book, but otherwise we teach . . . oh . . . do we? do we teach? ah, but . . . my god . . . what? what do we teach?

Unamuno was exiled to the Canaries for criticizing his country's dictator, but returned when it was made a republic. An elected official for a while, the philosopher concluded his public career by denouncing both the republic and its opposition. That's the ticket. Imagine a philosopher, today, of Unamuno's range of experience, Unamuno's knowledge, Unamuno's depth of understanding, Unamuno's style, Unamuno's quality of mind, Unamuno's beautiful name.

Yes, how important we are, we argue, when applying for government assistance; how impotent and barren, we allege our efforts are, when blamed for some abuse; and how much we should like to have it both ways: yet writers get it both ways these days only from the religious right, which is adept at striking every cheek—ass and face with the same slap—even if their adeptness tends to end with this, because their interest is bent on remaining ignorant, in the dark, and unchanged, so that they can continue to believe that *Huckleberry Finn, Slaughterhouse Five*, and *Catcher in the Rye* corrupt their youth. They must therefore strike their enemies without looking at them, as it were, from their own blind side, and with blows that do not bruise the very stones they've thrown.

Yet the religious right, whether we are speaking of it as it operates here in the United States, or as it exists in Muslim countries, or in other benighted areas around the world, cannot make the least headway, as out of date as they are, blinded by fanaticism and crippled by superstition, if they do not have the quiet compliance and tacit assistance of many in the so-called open, liberal, and modern world. If the Salman Rushdie case teaches us anything, it should warn us of the immense submerged sympathy for the *fatwa*, not only among the rest of the world's religions, which find here a common cause even if they lack the courage to claim it, but among every shrill and posturing minority that fear for their feelings if not for anyone else's, and therefore sympathize with the tenderness of other skins, so long, of course, as such sensitivities offer no threat to themselves.

Vissi d'arte, vissi d'amore, the soprano sings. Work or world, the tenor might wonder. No one, today, talks much about the conflict between art and lawnmowing, art and childbirth, art and marital disorders, art and parenthood, art and car downpayments. If a novel devotes itself to labor union organizing, munitions makers, or woolen manufacture, it would almost certainly be seen as a work of propaganda, perhaps high-minded, but "committed" nevertheless, for why else would one write about such things? My parents, or yours, are unquestioned subjects, and if I have an ax to grind about my second marriage, and the lout spouse I got stuck with, that's okay; what's fiction for? and if I write a series of lyrics about shopping at the supermarket, or planting a tree, or my vacation in the Rockies, these subjects aren't a problem either, my poems remain poems; but if I write another series on El Salvador, or about my sojourn in Siberia, my poems will inevitably be seen as political, partisan, apologia for this view or that movement, which may be okay, too, except that they cannot be approached merely as poems now, and kissed upon their kindly open face.

Once, as this recital suggests, art and the artist were part of the great world, but now art is only an alternative. Once, if a poet caused offense, it was as often as not for the way he had cast a vote, or advised a prince; and, once, if a poem offended, it was often because it charged the crown with a crime, or called certain courtiers to account. In the West, at any rate, there are now no princes of note for poets to know, and no public that might know a poet, and risk being moved. After the art, there is only the rest of the world. The rest of the world is nowadays roughly divided into two realms: the public and the private. The private is presumed to be art's special province, because the wide public world is far from any normal writer's ken, as remote as the High Command is for most of us.

The writer has the *Times* delivered daily, and there she can read about war and starvation and disease and the pillage of the planet, but what does she know first-hand about oiling an M-1 or international diplomacy or prison life in Sri Lanka; so, naturally, she is expected to write about what she knows best: getting a husband, keeping him happy, raising kids, getting on with the in-laws, aging without anxiety, going back to work, getting fat, finding time to read, burying her folks. And she frequently, dutifully does . . . write about that. However, when we observe that writers write about what most takes up their time, about what day to day impinges upon them most intimately, about what gets under their several skins—worries them, pleases, disappoints, we should also remember to place some considerable stress on the phrase, "takes up their time." It would be a grave mistake to suppose that it was only public life that intruded on the writer's work, imperiled it with its oppositions, or lured an otherwise secure and faithful art onto the path of partisanship, and entrapped it in the wiles of local social relevance, never to raise a worthy head again. Not only is "private" or domestic life larded throughout with public elements, it is as consuming as a fire, and composed of buttoning buttons, boiling water, cold toast eaten as if each chew were being counted, as well as long moments of mental vacancy filled by films, alcohol, hobbies and other habits of escape, and family quarrels so silly they create their own anger—in sum—by total trivialities and the bourgeois comforts of the self; which is why Villiers de L'Isle-Adam remarked, "As for living, we'll let our servants do that for us." The writer's greatest enemy is her subject, which she writes about in order to stave off its demands, expose its nullity, control its course, explain its character, to justify a marriage, vilify a husband, understand a child; just as writers wrote, in greater days, of plots to overthrow thrones, ways to get ahead, as well as those ill-starred love affairs that deterred one, tragically, from greater goals.

When Zhang Jie wrote a few stories championing romantic love over marriages traditionally arranged, the state chastised her, and such a cloud hung over her future she needed to seek safety abroad. The relation runs equally strongly the other way: the public world is everywhere infected by the private, and some suspect that the politics of the family is only too often repeated in the hierarchies of both church and state.

How to measure the fear of imprisonment and the displeasure of the state against the distractions of one's household and the irritation of a spouse, as well as the anxieties produced when lives are joined and jointly threaten, when families are shattered by jail or divorce, children orphaned or sent away, property confiscated or divided, hopes dimmed, and one is made homeless by events? Or, on the art, the consequence? A play is closed by the order of the king, and the playwright falls silent forever; a child dies, and the world receives an ode. For his nonpolitical position, Pasternak's poetry is banned, so he translates Shakespeare. During the war years, two volumes of poetry slip into print. But he is forced to decline the Nobel Prize, really given him for *Doctor Zhivago*, really given him for political reasons, really written from private grief, and shaped by history's course.

Francis Parkman was born to be a dilettante: rich, talented in an acceptably tepid way, with an unpleasant dependence on Haavaard and Baston and tea well-served, appropriately opposed to abolitionists, women's suffrage, the Democratic party, and money grubbing. He was, in these senses, dangerously parochial and a frightful snob, but instead of playing polo, he rode West, and saw what he saw with dispassionate clarity, and read what he read when he researched the French and Indian Wars with a devotion to fact that carried him straight through to values. It freed him to be La Salle, Champlain, Montcalm. Proust didn't have a prince who would comfortably confine him, so he put himself out of harm's way; and who knows how many other tribulations have been literary blessings, and how many of Nobel's prizes, or similar successes, have wrought havoc and complacency?

If you want to be made a fool of—take sides, and then let the side take you. This does not mean that all sides are, in moral sum, the same, for some are simply despicable, some are sordid, some are creatively stupid, many are criminally naive, most are poorly expressed, badly led, weakly implemented, and, underneath, up-to-no-good the moment they get organized; but when the sides are as general and vague as "life" and "art," or "literature" and "politics," it maybe useful to remember that coins and paper have sides, but value and language haven't; there are no sides to a stew, either, only surfaces, ingredients, and flavors. Of course, seated before the fire in one's dressing gown, as was Descartes's famous habit, wondering whether one is awake or dreaming, a bit brandied and full of a fine dinner, one is inclined to take Bobbie Burns's brief blunt way with things and say:

> The Kirk an' State may join, an' tell
> To do sic things I mauna:
> The Kirk an' State may gae to hell
> And I'll gae to my Anna.

The Writer in Politics

2   The Book Show

Antonio Skármeta

■ Antonio Skármeta is our distinguished writer-in-residence in
the Department of Romance Languages at Washington University. I should start by pointing out why he is one of the two or
three writers in my country, Chile, we look to for orientation, for
wisdom, for quality in literature. His first books, *El entusiasmo*
and *Desnudo en el tejado*, were provocative at a time of depres-
sion, when we were all existentialists, when we read Camus and
Sartre. These stories were new, daring, and innovative and took
place in what we call today a postmodern world of politics. They
opened a new dimension and created an imaginative world in
which we felt we could live better.

Antonio continued this innovation in his subsequent work. In
I Dreamt the Snow Was Burning, a young man from the south of
Chile wants to become a sports star. He discovers that he is becoming part of a much greater team, one that politically trans-
forms the country in the period right before Salvador Allende
was elected president in 1970; then he lives through the period
in which our history took a bad turn and we ended up in a dictatorship.

His novel *Burning Patience* became an instant classic; the
movie version has been seen by millions. This beautiful book, an
example of literary renaissance, combines the language, vision,
and memory of the great poet Pablo Neruda with a deep meditation on how a writer can be involved both in politics and in the
humble life of a people in a village on the coast of Chile.

His most recent novel, *Match Ball*, is a post-modern *Lolita*,
that seems to be about sex but is concerned with many other issues implicit in and tangential to sexuality.

He is also a film director; he has written many scripts that have
received great acclaim, and he has produced many movies and
plays for German television while he was an exile in Berlin. Lately,

he has returned to live in Chile. Today he is the first of the stars in the great constellation we have assembled here.

RANDOLPH POPE, *Moderator*

The Book Show

In 1969 the Chilean leftist parties could not agree on a single candidate for the 1970 elections. Sick and tired of the division in the populace, the Communist Party announced that if the others could not agree, they would present the poet Pablo Neruda as their candidate. The confusion continued, and Pablo Neruda did in fact become the candidate. In my novel *Burning Patience* I imagine Neruda receiving the news of his nomination in his refuge of Isla Negra, standing in front of his mailman who sees him turn pale upon reading the telegram.

"Bad news?" he asks.

"Horrendous," answers the poet. "They are offering me to be the nominee for the presidency."

"But, Don Pablo," the mailman gets emotional, "that's fantastic."

Neruda answers with a sigh: "Fantastic to become a candidate, but . . . what if I'm elected!"

"Naturally you will be elected! Everybody knows you. In our house my father has one of your books."

"And what does that prove?"

"What do you mean? If my father who doesn't know how to read or write has a book of yours in our house, that means we will win."

This dialogue charts a small route in the direction I would like to develop at this meeting on "The Writer in Politics." What makes a writer have political clout, and, indeed, so much of it that, when parties are cornered or desperate, they will turn to him? The opposite does not seem to occur, to have the writer search for the party in order to propel his career. If a political party comes searching for an author, it is not because he is in the process of seeking fame, but because he has already achieved it.

Writers who are still in the running are placed in the diplomatic corps or sent out of the country as ambassadors or cultural attachés. With this ploy, the politicians are doubly pleased: they satisfy the vanity of the writer and they remove him from the minefield of the deep political structure of the country, where the intellectual—who measures everything with a less pragmatic stick than the politician— can quickly become a complainer, then a disaffected person, and then an opponent and, finally, a prisoner.

What are the traits that politicians see in writers that make them seek them out and introduce them into the stew of politics? In the first place, they perceive in the writer something that they themselves are not; which is to say, a public person whose prestige transcends parties, having an aura that surpasses his ties with a party or with an ideology; a voice that speaks to a wider audience because it does not eschew the complexity of the real, simplifying it to attain immediate goals, but rather, possessed of a privileged technical expression, it is capable of communicating the weight, color, historical dimension, perspectives, the very emotion of reality. And it not only interprets and illuminates reality, it also introduces fantastic products into that reality which are worlds in words, as William H. Gass calls them. Neruda, who in some moments of his life was dithyrambic vis-à-vis some tough patriarchs, and who was more communist than was prudent, won the hearts of Chileans, not because he invoked old Whitman in order to help him kill Nixon in a continental conspiracy, but because he taught Chileans to see their wind, their sea, their fish; because he convinced the lowliest worker that he could be material for poetry; because he put us in touch with the marvel of eating a fish stew, of the native civilization hidden right under our feet—buried rather ("Rise and be born with me, brother")—of the erotic words which, whispered into the ears of young women, can lead to great pleasures.

Such is the stuff of literary success; it is what propels the intellectual away from his normal sphere, a curious deed since there would be no reason to think that a writer who understands his people, who criticizes them, loves them, interprets them, and reveals their symbols and traumas to them, could in addition be their leader. It is true that he has shown proof of intelligence, and has certainly come into conflict with the materialistic interests of great segments of the population, but does that in itself make the writer an administrative leader? Or might a writer think that his enormous aesthetic and moral prestige will confer on him the authority that diverse national and international forces will accept without questioning his wishes when he proposes political measures that might affect different segments of the population? The answer in Latin America is clearly no. Those writers who have become presidents have been uniformly unseated; or rather, before taking office, they have been exiled. Still, to have been overthrown and exiled is excellent preparation to be elected president again.

In order to speak of great writers, recent cases are relevant. Rómulo Gallegos was elected president of Venezuela on December 14, 1947, with 870,000 votes out of 1,183,000. Gallegos, the author of *Doña Bárbara*, explained his motives for engaging in politics in banking language: "I am a loan from literature to politics on a fixed short-term basis." In his acceptance speech before a multitude that adored him, Gallegos changed the terms of his deposit: "It happened that from that loan, instead of recovering my personal autonomy, I earned lasting profit in that . . . one belongs to oneself the more one puts one's thought and will, one's whole life on behalf of a collective idea . . . I do not lend anything; rather I receive and accept: honor and responsibility." Neruda felt some of the same emotions when it befell him to be a nominee for the presidency: "I learned much from the sea and its waves, but much more from the tenderness of a thousand eyes looking at me at the same time." Nine months later Rómulo Gallegos was unseated in a coup commanded by Marcos Pérez Jiménez.

Thus ended the political career of a writer that began with the enormous success of *Doña Bárbara*. The novel had fallen into the hands of the dictator in power at the time of its publication. Juan Vicente Gómez wanted to read it because some troublemakers had whispered to him that the novel was an attack against him. Dr. Requena, the dictator's secretary, told essayist Juan Liscano that he personally had read the novel to the dictator in his hacienda. When night fell, the secretary suggested that they stop reading because of the darkness, but the dictator was so taken with the work that Requena had to read it by the light of the headlights at night. When he finished, the dictator observed: "This is not against me, because it is too good. This is what writers ought to do instead of taking part in goddamned revolutions." From that moment on, friends of the dictator and of Gallegos tried to get both of them together and to enlist Gallegos in the government. Gómez named Gallegos minister of education in order to placate the students.

There is no better candidate for the presidency in Latin America than one who has been a candidate and lost. It is better than to have been a candidate and won, since several constitutions forbid a second term. The previous experience gets the candidate ready for the next election. Our colleague Mario Vargas Llosa claims that he has learned from this fact, and will not run again. I do not doubt his intentions, nor the capacity of politicians to change the mind of the most wise of mortals, and to convince them that it is necessary "to sacrifice oneself for the fatherland." This tradition of being an eternal candidate was followed by none other than our Salvador Allende, who was elected president of Chile on his fourth try. Allende himself had proposed his epitaph: "Here lies Salvador Allende, future president of Chile."

The Sandinista revolution in Nicaragua achieved an interesting array of support in its insurrectional phase thanks to the broad spectrum of forces, from liberal to Marxist, as well as because some of its leaders were writers. Sergio Ramírez, who was vice-president, had received his doctorate in exile, and Ernesto Cardenal saw the revolution in Nicaragua as a fragment of a cosmic liberation in which revolution is a form of love, a feeling better expressed by poetry than by laws. From the Ministry of Education, Cardenal fulfilled the desire of the rebellious victors for poetry by creating literary workshops throughout Nicaragua. He achieved a rare miracle by having the best workshop be the one with the police! Cardenal searched in pre-Hispanic America for precedents with which to fight the power of money and of postmodern liberalism. He thus found the kingdom of a poet, Netzahualcóyotl, to whom he dedicated enthusiastic verses in *Homenaje a los indios Americanos* (*Homage to the American Indians*):

> A pacifist king who has not come to earth to wage war
> but to cut flowers,
> and whose palace is full of singers and not of soldiers,
> who organizes literary contests under the trees,
> whose court is "melancholy,"
> who was not in favor of human sacrifices,

and whose greatest pleasure was to utter "some true
words among the objects which perish."
Poets came to Texcoco,
modern painters to paint murals,
and intellectuals from Tenochtitlán came running away
from the land where the military burned books.

Cardenal's very beautiful poem ought to be contrasted with the rigors of history, which explains perhaps why writers are used by politicians as victorious standards that are then dropped to the ground like a kite without wind. History tells us that when Montezuma assumed power in Tenochtitlán, the site of modern Mexico City, Netzahualcóyotl was ordered to recognize him as the supreme monarch of the universe. The pacifist monarch did this, but Tlacaellel, Montezuma's adviser, suggested that such a show of vassalage was not enough, that he had to be defeated in combat in order to suit the Aztecs. According to R. C. Padden, the documents indicate that the adviser suggested that the Aztecs inflict pain and bloodletting on the enemy so others "would feel terror knowing that we have destroyed the temple of Texcoco." Thus one arrived at the first act of magic realism, curiously not fictionalized by either Gabriel García Márquez or Cecil B. De Mille. A major battle with thousands of extras was put on, and then Netzahualcóyotl had to put fire to the temple himself, to swear allegiance to the new gods, and to provide victims for the sacrifices made of real flesh and bone. I don't think that in the history of mankind there has existed a greater humiliation of a poet, nor a greater metaphor for the defeat of a pacifist utopia, of the language of concord, of the impotence of art to establish other words than those of military and political jargon.

Unfortunately, the colleagues who achieve the presidency are few, and Vaclav Havel's experience in Czechoslovakia shows us that such things don't last long.* André Malraux under Charles de Gaulle and Jorge Semprun under Felipe Gonzalez occupied posts which had to do with culture, and in those delimited spaces they excelled. The acceptance of defeat by the Sandinistas, on the other hand, leaves them in a hopeful position and with full accreditation for the future, having

---

Editor's note: At the time of this talk, Czechoslovakia had voted to split into two countries and Vaclav Havel had handed in his resignation as president of that country.

evinced the downfall of Socialism. Sergio Ramírez emerges as one of our colleagues destined to play a primary role in the future of Nicaragua.

The fact that people and politicians attribute to writers a greater sensitivity to understand a country, its history, its landscape; a greater flexibility to love difference and to protect it; a certain lack of moral contamination; and a language that does not fall into the clichés of political discourse, creates a situation which writers might call love-hate. A writer is appreciated to the degree that he subscribes meekly to a political group, while the members celebrate—paradoxically—the prestige lent by his originality and independence. But if this colleague diverges from the broad outlines of the political and moral action of these political parties, then they do not hesitate to attack virulently the writer's errors. A whole international conspiracy was mounted against Neruda when he went to New York for a PEN meeting, because on the return flight he stopped to have breakfast with then president of Peru Fernando Belaúnde Terry. "So much fuss because of a pair of fried eggs," said Neruda bitterly.

If we concentrate on the distress that many colleagues in this audience must have endured, one can infer that if the writer turns out to be uncomfortable in a democracy because of what Nadine Gordimer called "the artist's rebellious integrity to the state of being manifest in life around her or him," it is under the power of dictatorships that this marginality and rebellion attain a very dangerous level. The writer is now entitled, perhaps for the first time in his life, to the attention of the state, which bestows upon him repeated threats, punishment in the hands of thugs, prison, exile, *desaparición* (disappearance), and even assassination.

· Chilean writers, who confronted a merciless dictatorship between 1973 and 1989, quite urgently found images to give cohesion to a society fragmented and immobilized by military terrorism. Before we could write one critical line in Chile, or even proclaim a proven fact in the manipulated, sold-out, and cynical media, it was the playwrights who established images of pain as well as compassion, in which the victims recognized their terror during the day, but also recognized the whisper of that which, albeit decimated or fragmented, would not dissolve into anguish or acquiescence.

Many actors and playwrights received death threats, their playhouses were destroyed, and they had to take short vacations away from Chile to weather the storm. Except that now—as in the case of Salman Rushdie—the government was confronted by the international response of renowned authors in defense of their assailed colleagues. With the regime now in agony, actors and authors created open images of rebellion, produced a contagious excitement, and as many as forty of them were threatened with death unless they left the country. But none of them did. Instead, they solicited international solidarity, and immensely popular colleagues traveled to Chile. The United States Actors Guild sent Christopher Reeve, then very well known in Chile for his recent role as Superman. The most important newspaper of the opposition printed the headline: "Superman has come to save us from Pinochet."

I am convinced that an alliance between politics and writers can produce healthy tensions and benefit the country. I say this because of my own experience in two very different situations in which poets participated in the design of a political fiction that contributed to the fall of Pinochet. In 1988, after fifteen years of government, the dictator decided to normalize the situation in Chile, and take the country out of its international isolation by calling a referendum in which the people were asked to vote on his presidency for eight more years. Most people reacted with skepticism and bitterness, since more than once the dictator had called a referendum, had counted the votes at home, and had proclaimed himself a winner, almost always by a modest margin of seventy-five percent in his favor.

This time, however, the opposition obtained permission from the government to have delegates in the voting places, and the government—with incredible arrogance—also allowed them ten minutes on television at night to present their point of view. The program was titled "*La franja del No*"—The Space for a No-Vote—due to its commitment to clearly say "No More" to the dictatorship. Pinochet, opening for the first time such a popular and tightly controlled medium of communication, was not counting on a postmodern phenomenon. The writers who had been fired from their jobs at the university, the film makers who had survived the concentration camps, the graphic designers who had been prosecuted because of their political ideas, had sold their talents to advertising agencies, the only business in which they could work and survive without going into exile. These commercial artists knew quite well a market where anything could be sold, and where Chile was celebrated as a consumer's paradise. Now, for the first time, they could market a product that did not belong to the prosperous entrepreneurs, but had to do with their deepest emotions: No to Pinochet. Working for the agencies, they had learned the techniques of synthesis, sensual seduction, conceptual concentration, communicability. They only needed to infuse the message with a poetic spirit; they had to perceive what to tell people who were terrified, leery of the whole process of the referendum, apathetic. Script writers—and there were acclaimed authors among them—jumping from the underground to the foreground of massive public view, had to adopt a clear-cut, yet ironic inflection, the favorite tool of the Chilean people to face with laughter the tombstone that alienated them from confidence and fraternity. Instead of reiterating the pathetic laments that the regime anticipated, the Chilean writers launched a campaign under the slogan: "Chile, happiness is forthcoming!" Thus, our writers invented what I have termed— with a small dose of humor—"poetic publicity." The results were spectacular: the images created by these artists most certainly did not organize the resistance movement that had been working arduously from the first day of the military coup in 1973, but they did encourage the people to vote without fear. Space now opened to the No-Vote, destabilizing the dictatorship's self-promotion apparatus.

Indeed every political movement that is conducive to a life of truth, and to an authentic conduct, has previously been a melting pot of impressions, feelings, common dissatisfactions, impotent behavior, resentments, memories, frustrations, and desires. This amorphous melting pot is precisely privileged ground for the writer. From it, the writer conceives his characters, and fashions their behavior. From it, he proposes values, criticizes, and offers encouragement and discouragement. Politicians, on the other hand, model their positions—and their oppositions—in an attempt to diminish the potential of the rich brew they must reduce to a simple schema. Literature's most political act vis-à-vis all citizens is to get them used to sharing the complexities of their world and to make them highly suspicious of any school of thought that tends to simply outline the perplexing spectacle of reality, in order to force it into submission to mediocre interpretations and rigid cogitations. I do not see from which other perspective, save that of art, all citizens could develop the habit of irony, which is often the only possibility of rebellion for the intelligentsia.

And since we have highlighted the work of intellectuals who, in a particular political circumstance, subverted the marketing habits of the televised media by using a truly communicative language, we must also assert that one of the political functions of literature is to work as the counterpart to the enormous deficiencies of the media, generally domesticated by the impositions of a rating system, the moral prerequisites of the state, and the robot-like apportionment of common sense. The media's hegemonic discourse not only does not enlighten with what little it exhibits, it also reveals the powerful absence of all that is hushed because it is not a matter of public consumption.

That explains the total desperation of writers when they face the programming of television, the ongoing complaint that their profession is in a state of prolonged agony due to the rapid spread of the banality prevailing in the media, so capable of stifling the development of a critical conscience in the viewing audience. One ineffectual possibility is to rejoice in those complaints, and find consolation in the complicity and loyalty of the cultured reading minorities. Another strategy is to open the language used in television, endowing it with other signifiers, bringing in what is heterogeneous and even marginal, doing battle in the minefields where the monster rejoices, making new images breathe.

Soon after I returned from exile, I perceived that the new democracy had adopted a complacent attitude. Everything that was somewhat dissonant had a very low profile. As far as the press was concerned, the intellectual elite would observe, with no small dose of sarcasm, the amnesia of the immediate past, and the frivolity with which the media reiterated facile entertainment quite similar to what prevailed during the years of dictatorship. There was freedom of expression, but such freedom was exercised to say very little, and even that seemed to be useless rhetoric. The writers were afraid that within the new order, effective restlessness would stagnate.

> If modernity is not only a culture of efficiency, and if democracy is not to be only the preservation of a State of Law and the ritualization of political competence, there will always be an intellectual on the other side of the power structure—and against those who seek power—beyond

state or academic institutionalization. There will always be
the intellectual asking seemingly facetious questions, rein-
terpreting controversy by making it reappear, in order to
show that the questioning of that which might not be a
part of the public agenda, or might be subtly suppressed
by the media is still legitimate. (Richard 1992)

To sum up, what was happening was something that might bring
a smile to the faces of some of my colleagues in the audience, who
have faced rigorous repression in their own countries, or perhaps have
endured a prolonged situation of exile. It was an enormous paradox:
the writers felt that the impact of their work was much more significant under harsh conditions of repression than under the present
circumstances of democratic bliss.

I do believe that an appropriate response to these apprehensions
lies in the understanding of the nonutopic character of democracy.
That is to say, the absence of purpose in all democratic regimes, the
nonexistence of a breaking point from which definite goals will be
reached—as in socialism, communism, communitarianism, or perfect
competence—provokes the bewilderment of the Latin American intellectuals, because they have to modify their discourse in light of
what is possible. Democracy is always a process, and as such it contains
a dose of imprecision and hybridism that makes possible its continuous quest for perfection. Even more than a utopia, democracy is a
strategy to organize social life. Thus, within a democracy, where all
conflicts are regulated by consensus, the act of protest lacks any trau-
matic profile. The challenge for writers is to comprehend, enlarge,
and imagine those specific problems that trouble people.

And it is here that I want to state that the commonplace is also a
shared fallacy. I am a writer who derives pleasure from framing his
characters within the problems of his own lifetime, and as a citizen
it is my vocation not to accept the repressed language that society
prescribes. I am a naive believer in literature as a praxis not only of
fantasy but also of freedom, since the person who has walked many
paths will be the only one to discern which path will be chosen to
go home.

Thus I pondered, after my return to Chile from exile, whether perhaps what I wanted most was to use the enormous popularity of the
media to implement subtle changes from within, and I proposed to

the proper authorities in charge of the national television—a state organization—a series dedicated to books and authors. Its main objective would be to lure the viewing audience, quite removed now from the written text, into the practice of reading books. That was my political project within the new Chilean democratic horizon. I intended to broaden the limits of public fantasy by revealing the originality of the writers' viewpoints, their knowledge, their irony, their pain, and their eccentricities. Those I approached at the network acknowledged my project with the same happiness that must have overcome Socrates upon swallowing hemlock. The Chilean channels compete for ratings, and anything that departs from a homogenous and proven formula is viewed as senseless, only conducive to a loss of viewers and—sadder yet—rich commercial sponsors. At the same time, the charge that television, with its fascination for visual images, had put literature in a coma, seemed to weigh heavily on their souls. A literary program conceived by a writer just back from exile seemed like a democratic variant that fulfilled the purpose of cultural dissemination so fitting for a television channel. We agreed to a three-month weekly series, in half-hour episodes, with a ridiculously low budget, to air at 11:00 in the evening, a time slot most convenient for those suffering from insomnia, for sleepwalkers, and for owls. When I protested and tried to schedule my program at a time more suitable for most human beings, one of the directors swiftly remarked: "Not to worry! Nobody will see your program anyway. . . . The most successful cultural program we've ever aired had a 3 percent rating."

Uplifted by the director's optimism, I worked with a team of literature enthusiasts and filmmakers quite eager to see different images and combinations of images than the conventional ones on television. After months of work the program opened, strategically named "El Show de los Libros" (The book show).

I must say that I am somewhat proud of what eventually happened, as I was one of the creators of the program, but I tell the story in this symposium on writers and politics to stress the significance of the event, and not the relative importance of any participant. The literary program started with a 5 percent rating. The second week it obtained 8 percent, then 17 percent, and it kept on climbing until the eleventh transmission when it hit 36 percent, the same rating usually captured by star-studded programs with million-dollar budgets.

Dissidence in its way of showing and telling was unexpectedly producing an alliance between intellectuals tired of the status quo and the viewing audience allegedly addicted to the banality of everyday programming. Perhaps this was only a fortuitous circumstance, even a one-time affair, but the reception of these normal citizens to a different type of program led me to doubt those well-established notions about the psychology of a mass audience, and also to question the definition of normality endorsed by politicians.

Hans Magnus Enzensberger, in his ironic essay *Political Crumbs*, defends normal people, stating: "As far as the species is capable of surviving, it will presumably owe its continued existence not to some outsiders or other but to quite normal people." The political utopia that is left for us writers is this alliance between normality and marginality. Yet, these meeting spaces are not simply given away or even desirable to those in charge of political administration. We must search for them, we must fight for them, we must defend them once they are conquered, and we must learn to abandon them when they become stale. In fact, I cannot see why we writers must lead normal people into the hands of those politicians. In not doing so lies our moral and political responsibility.

Panel Discussion
Panelists: Marc Chénetier, Carolyn Forché,
James McLeod, Randolph Pope, Mario Vargas Llosa

Randolph Pope: I'm sure that all of us, marginal and normal, enjoyed this lecture. Mario, are you considering coming back a second time?

Mario Vargas Llosa: No, certainly not. But I shall keep participating in politics, writing about it, debating, proposing some goals. This, I think, is something a writer should do, and not only in countries with enormous problems as most Latin American countries have, but also in advanced democracies. I think it's necessary to have, in a healthy democratic society, participation from intellectuals, writers, and artists, people who are supposed to work in the realm of ideas and imagination, and not let politics become completely controlled by stereotypes, by maneuvering, by intrigues, and by very limited and mediocre goals. I think writers can bring something to politics if they use their imagination, and their preoccupation with words and discourse, which is essential to illuminate for people the real problems and the real world. My impression is that one of the reasons for the mediocrity so common to the political field in advanced democracies is a lack of participation, because politics has become the monopoly of a professional class. People now feel cynical or totally skeptical about the possibility of change and about using the political institutions in a society. On the other hand, I don't think that it is good for a society to believe, as has been the case in Latin America and many third world countries, that a writer, because he is a writer, has better insight or more authority to give opinions and answers on political matters. This romantic idea of what a writer is, is still very strong in Latin America. That is the reason writers are so pressured in our countries to give opinions and answers not only on politics but on everything; and that is the reason why writers usually enjoy this moral authority, this respectability, which in some cases explains why they are targeted by dictatorships and are victims of persecution. There is this idea that the writer can produce important changes. I think this is wrong, but I think a writer can give us a very rich and interesting perspective with which to analyze or to discuss political problems. Culture and politics are, or should be, intimately linked, and this is something a writer faces in his daily work. From this point of view, I think the writer can give testimony to the importance of culture in the political debate and in the political development of society.

Randolph Pope: But writers can be wrong.

Mario Vargas Llosa: In Latin America, where there is this tradition of participation of writers in politics, something which I think is good, we have to balance the options that writers have promoted. Writers in Latin America have attacked progressive ideas and values. In many cases writers have been accomplices to nasty and negative political operations. Even in the nineteenth century, for instance, probably the best prose writer of Latin America, Domingo Sarmiento, the author of a fantastic book called *Facundo* and a very good translator of Dante, provided the ethical and cultural justification for the genocide of the Indians in Argentina. He was convinced that the only way that

Argentina and Latin America could be modern was to eliminate the pre-Spanish culture, namely the barbarians. The result of that was military invasions and genocide. In modern times in Latin America, great writers have not promoted tolerance, pluralism, coexistence, diversity, and democratic options. They have promoted revolution and glamorized socialism, communism, and collectivism. Neruda, probably the greatest Latin America poet in modern times, wrote poems in favor of Stalin even though he was critical of right-wing military dictatorships. And Borges, our best Spanish-speaking prose writer, accepted a decoration from Pinochet without any scruples. So I think writers in Latin America have been on the wrong side in many cases. We must also take this into consideration when we think about the commitment of the writer in Latin America, something which I think is good, but which also must be judged by what the writers have promoted and defended.

Randolph Pope: I wonder, Marc Chénetier, in France, when Mitterand took over, if he also believed in what Antonio was saying—about the importance of imagination. He brought together hundreds of intellectuals. Did that have any impact on French life, Mitterand's vision of culture?

Marc Chénetier: In the French tradition the very definition of an intellectual presupposes a certain distance and opposition. When the people you have supported for a long time finally come to power, you feel as if you've been pushing against a door and all of a sudden the door is opened and you fall on your face. Even so, I don't think that the poet or the intellectual or the thinker *at any moment* should be on the side of the powers that be, even if the people they have been supporting come to power. I think this is a sort of *a contrario* demonstration of the function of intellectuals. Intellectuals voice ideas; it is against the grain of writers to voice ideas as such. Therefore, I think we should differentiate among the strands of our conversation here.

What I was very grateful for in Antonio's paper is that he opened up the old notion that the writer's importance is message-oriented. Yesterday, Mario, you gave us this reading from a book that you described as an attempt at linking eroticism, literature, and painting. I think that there is an erotic connection here: writers cannot adopt the missionary position. The minute it becomes a transitive tool, the very notion of what writing *is* collapses because it has to pander to acceptability of discourse. I think that the poetic text (in the larger sense), is, as Barthes would put it, "that carefree person that shows his behind to the political father." When one tries to reach a wider audience, one actually disrupts the quality and the power of one's own writing. I would much rather go Antonio's way and read in this relationship that exists between politics and writing, what he described as dream bubbles in a minefield. Whatever cleanses the language is a hygienic activity that rids the political discourse of the miasma generated by the political activity—which is transitive discursively. To me it is more important to open up language and to show its possibilities, to demonstrate how it can be manipulated so that people will know that it is being manipulated. The fictions that are being built are as powerful as any transitive political tool. I'd much rather go along with someone else you quote, Antonio, Enzensberger, when he talks about writing being the consciousness industry. There is this notion that until people have seen the way that you can build these worlds of fiction (because what is a political program but one of the most extraordinary fictions that you have to sell?), that's the way reality is going to be read. If you propose alternative fictions, you are doing much more efficient work than pushing any sort of political program.

Randolph Pope: But isn't there a space in which to give voice to the violence in El Salvador, as Joan Didion and Carolyn Forché have done? Or in the case, I imagine, of the violence in our own inner cities, and the problems that we had in Los Angeles? Isn't it a function of writers to do that, in the same way Mario did with *La guerra del fin del mundo* (*The War of the End of the World*), a way in which one can bring these things from the margins to the center? Would any of you like to comment on this? Carolyn?

Carolyn Forché: When I listen to Antonio's speech and Mario's reactions, I reflect on the differences between their experience as writers in Latin America and our experience as writers in the United States. We don't get sent abroad in diplomatic posts. When I was first invited to El Salvador, they wanted to have a North American poet learn as much as possible about the situation there before the war began, so that *when* the war began (as I was told quite explicitly), this poet could come back to the United States and speak to the American people about the reasons for it because the North Americans' opinions were going to be critical to the outcome. First I asked, "Do you know how poets are viewed in the United States?" They said, "No, how?" So I tried to explain our marginality. I said that we're a fringe element. We don't have a great deal of credibility. We are bohemians or we're mentally ill or we commit suicide or jump off bridges. Most North Americans cannot even name any poets. I said, "I don't think I am the proper messenger. Don't you want some sort of junior journalist, a young Barbara Walters, so that this person will come back and be listened to?" They said, "No, we want a poet or writer, someone who has a sensitivity and critical distance, someone who can awaken language." And I was told by Salvadorans, "If this is your situation as a writer in the United States, then you must change this. Americans must not view writers in this way." So I thought, "Oh yes, I'm not only going to explain the war in El Salvador, I'm also going to change the position of writers and poets in the United States!"

Right after Vaclav Havel became president of Czechoslovakia, he traveled to Washington and gave an address before Congress. The address was riveting. There was a very positive bipartisan reaction. Some of the senators later said, "Why don't we ever have language like that? Why don't we ever hear political speeches like that? Why don't we have that quality of linguistic engagement in our political process?" It occurred to several of us that it may be because Vaclav Havel actually wrote the speech himself and that what Americans were listening to for the first time in a long while was the sustained voice of a human being rather than a committee of speech writers, political analysts, and marketers, cobbling something together that would please everyone and no one. Vaclav Havel was received very warmly because of his moral authority, the quality of his speech, his language; it was clear, forthright, honest, and critical. We are so unaccustomed to that.

I subsequently traveled to Czechoslovakia, where an assistant of his, a journalist, Eda Kriseová said, "One thing we don't have time to do around here is write. Havel says that if we do the work and last even a few months then we will have something to write about for the rest of our lives." So everyone made notes and saved the material for later. The sad truth is that I think political life and the writer's life are so demanding that I don't know that they can be done simultaneously. Writers require solitude to sustain contemplation that I don't think is possible in political life. For myself, even going around and giving talks about the situation regarding human rights in El Salvador eroded my capacity to write. I had to make a decision: Which would be more important? Perhaps I decided wrongly. I decided for speaking in public. I realize now that what is left is a handful of poems. Perhaps we didn't accomplish anything. We didn't have much effect on the process.

Randolph Pope: I think that was Antonio's point, that writers may have a mysterious effect in generating images of hope or transformation.

Carolyn Forché: I hope so. Perhaps moral authority is ascribed to writers because we make our minds public. If we are honest, if we oppose tyranny, dictatorship, and the violation of human rights, it is a very public opposition. If we are people of integrity, we may find ourselves in situations where we're punished for that opposition. The accrual of moral integrity is probably the result of that process. All ordinary human beings have this same accrual of moral authority but with less visibility.

James McLeod: I was struck listening to Antonio's talk about the role of the poet. I am trying to think of it in an American context, as Carolyn has done. I thought of Bill Gass on a party ticket. Why not? Also I was struck by the words about democracy. When you move from the margins to the center in a democratic process, there is a diminished moral authority. You maintain that at the cost of those who are on the margins. I thought that the 3 percent rating for your first television program was very good. Somehow that was persuasive to me. You maintained something which you lose, perhaps, when you get 36 percent.

Randolph Pope: Antonio, would you care to comment on two points? One is that writers can be wrong when they create these imaginary ideas. Your perspective was a very optimistic one, and I'm very grateful for that. The other is that you may have been corrupted by going to 36 percent.

Antonio Skármeta: I would be pleased to be corrupted any time. Don't worry about it.

Randolph Pope: Why did this program become so popular? It is amazing. When you enter the mainstream, how do you continue to examine your positions? Tell us about the response to your show.

Antonio Skármeta: I told this story because I care very much about the alliance between intellectuals and "normal people." It has been my political purpose all of my life, not only to write in solitude and to be alone with my work, but also to act in society and not only with words. The reactions I had were from those who I don't think had ever read books. But they came to me on the street, always with the same kinds of speech: "You made me understand things that I never thought I could understand." That was surprising. I don't know if every country in North America is like this, but in Chile or Nicaragua I have seen some curious reactions: People have a very tender, very warm reaction to poetry, to literature, even if they have never read a book. One time in 1969 I saw Neruda campaigning in Chile. It was a very boring political speech, a very rainy day, and people were standing in the mud. When Neruda wanted to leave, they began to shout, "Poetry! Poetry! We want poetry!" And he asked, "What poems would you like me to read?" From these people came unexpectedly ten or twelve titles of different poems, and as he began to read one of them there came a chorus. I don't think these people had been to school! Writers have this aura, even though they make political mistakes, or are enthusiastic about some patriarchs who don't deserve our admiration. The fact is that there is a hunger for poetry.

Mario Vargas Llosa: This phenomenon that Antonio pointed out about Latin America comes from the nineteenth century, this romantic ideal of the poet as one who is inspired with answers for all kinds of problems. What happened in Chile with Neruda happened in France with Victor Hugo. He was considered not only a poet and novelist but a man with extraordinary powers to say the last word on social, moral, political, and cultural problems. I think there is something very naive in this, but on the other hand, it is also very moving. Behind the mythology of the poet is also the idea that writing or creating literature is not and should not be something gratuitous, something which has the goal of providing entertainment, but something very important that can help people solve their problems and enrich their lives. Behind this idea that the poet is some kind of moral authority or conscience for society is the idea that literature is important—that literature is not entertainment or an irresponsible game of the imagination, but something that can change your life.

Audience Member (Nuruddin Farah): I want to address my point to Vargas Llosa who seems to be full of confusion. On the one hand, he says politics is extremely boring; on the other hand, he says that poets are romantic idealists who do not know what they do. That seems to me to be one contradiction. The other is that Vargas Llosa pointed to genocide several times and to Neruda's failure to pay attention to Stalin's concentration camps. Neruda is accused of having been a communist sympathizer. Vargas Llosa points to some amorphous idea called "advanced democracy," which I presume to mean a society like the United States, but if one were a black person in a so-called advanced democracy, would one still consider it advanced? And the final question is: Do you not think that you are in fact doing what you are accusing Neruda of having done—that you are promoting an ideology based on wrong reasons as far as the masses are concerned?

Mario Vargas Llosa: It's a question that demands a long answer that I cannot provide, but I'll try to be very subjective. I think that people who have read what I have written know what kind of democracy I defend and promote. For many countries there is only one type of democracy, with different levels of perfection or imperfection. Then there are different kinds of dictatorships which I oppose, all of them: dictatorships represented by, for instance, Haiti now, or Peru, the fundamentalist Muslim dictatorships, the third world military dictatorships in Asia or Africa, the communist dictatorships in Korea and Cuba. I oppose all of this in the name of the Western liberal democratic society, which I think is a less imperfect organization of society—not the ideal society, that doesn't exist. Democracy is very imperfect in the United States, in Great Britain, in France, in Spain, and in Latin America where fortunately we have nineteen or twenty democratic, imperfect regimes.

My criticism of writers like Neruda is also a self-criticism because during the 1960s I was deeply committed to leftist causes that I think have been very damaging for Latin America and for the third world in general. I think we are now, at last, in Latin America, choosing the democratic option, and I think this is very good for the continent. But we have been losing time, so much so that we are now a very backward continent with tremendous social, economic, and cultural problems. For many years we were generally unable to see that the democratic system, with all its imperfections, was the system better prepared to reduce human rights abuses and political violence, and also the best system to provide development, economic progress, jobs, and opportunities for our countries. This has been the choice of people in Russia, in Central Europe, and is also the choice of Latin American people. My criticism is that intellectuals in Latin America—unlike those in Czechoslovakia, Poland, Russia, or China—were not, with exceptions, at the avant-garde of these movements for the democratization of the country, and against right-wing and left-wing totalitarianism and authoritarianism. On the contrary, in many cases our best writers, poets, and novelists were a major obstacle because they were providing glamour and beautification of everything that in the rest of the world was perceived as brutal dictatorship, marginalization of dissidents, intolerance for criticism, the destruction of individual freedom. In Latin America in many cases writers and poets were hiding from public opinion through sometimes very beautiful poems. I remember a poem by Ernesto Cardenal, which I heard myself, explaining that the kingdom of God was the communist society, that the communist society represented exactly the incarnation of the kingdom of God. What? No. After what has happened this cannot be accepted as a responsible play-game of a poet, but a very serious mistake, which, in a way, contributed to making democratization much more difficult in countries in which the tradition of violence has always been linked with intolerance and with dogma of different kinds of ideologies.

3   Politics and Literature: The Odd Couple

Mario Vargas Llosa

■ As a Latin Americanist, I was particularly fascinated by the comments made by Carolyn Forché earlier today about the differences between writers in North America and Latin America. Imagine a North American political rally and the crowd shouting for poetry! If the subject of poetry came up, if someone dared, you might be carried off bodily.

But now we have the distinct pleasure of welcoming Mario Vargas Llosa.

MARGARET SAYERS PEDEN, *Moderator*

Politics and Literature: The Odd Couple

The Peruvian novelist José María Arguedas killed himself the second day of December 1969 in a classroom of La Molina Agricultural University in Lima. He was a very discreet man and so as not to disturb his colleagues and the students with his suicide, he waited until everybody had left the place. Near his body was found a letter with very detailed instructions about his burial: where he should be mourned, who should pronounce the eulogies in the cemetery, and he asked, too, that an Indian musician friend of his play the *huaynos* and *mulizas* he was fond of. His will was respected and Arguedas, who had been, when he was alive, a very modest and shy man, had a very spectacular political burial.

But some days later other letters written by him appeared, little by little. They, too, were different aspects of his last will and they were addressed to very different people: his publisher, friends, journalists, academics, politicians. The main subject of these letters was his death,

60

of course, or better, the reasons for which he decided to kill himself. These reasons changed from letter to letter. In one of them, he said that he had decided to commit suicide because he felt that he was finished as a writer, that he no longer had the impulses and the will to create. In another, he gave moral, social, and political reasons: he could no longer stand the misery and neglect of the Peruvian peasants, those people of the Indian communities among whom he had been raised; he lived oppressed and anguished by the crisis of the cultural and educational life in the country; the low level and abject nature of the press and the caricature of liberty in Peru were too much for him, etc. . . .

In these dramatic letters, we follow, naturally, the personal crisis that Arguedas had been going through, and they are the desperate call of a suffering man who, at the edge of the abyss, asks mankind for help and compassion. But they are not only a clinical testimony. They are also graphic evidence of the situation of the writer in Latin America in the 1960s, of the difficulties and pressures of all sorts that had surrounded and oriented and many times destroyed the literary vocation in our countries.

In the United States and in Western Europe, to be a writer means, generally, first (and usually only) to assume a personal responsibility. That is, the responsibility to achieve in the most authentic way, a work which, for its artistic values and originality, enriches the language and culture of the country. In Peru, in Bolivia, in Nicaragua, on the contrary, to be a writer meant, until very recently, to assume a social responsibility: at the same time you developed a personal literary work, you were supposed to act, through your writing but also through your deeds, as a participant in the solution of the economic, political, and cultural problems of your society. There was no way to escape this obligation. If you tried to, if you were to isolate yourself and concentrate exclusively on your own work, you were severely censored and considered, in the best of cases, irresponsible and selfish; or, at worst, even by omission, an accomplice to all the evils of your country—illiteracy, misery, exploitation, injustice, prejudice—against which you had refused to fight. In the letters which he wrote when he had prepared the gun with which he was to kill himself, Arguedas was trying, in the last moments of his life, to fulfill this moral imposition that impelled all Latin American writers to social and political commitment.

Why was it like this? Why could not writers in Latin America until now be artists, and only artists? Why were they also obliged to be reformers, politicians, revolutionaries, moralists? The answer lies in the social conditions of Latin America, the problems that have faced our countries. All countries have problems, of course, but in many parts of Latin America, both in the past and even in the present, the problems that constitute the closest daily reality for people are not always freely discussed and analyzed in public, but are usually denied or silenced. Now, with the disappearance of dictators and the establishment of democracies in most Latin American nations, this has changed. But even in the recent past, there were no means through which those problems could be presented and denounced, because the social and political establishment exercised a strict censorship of the media and the communications systems. For example, if, in the 1970s or 1980s, you heard Chilean broadcasts or saw Argentine television, you would not hear a word about the political prisoners, about the exiles, about the torture, about the violations of human rights in those two countries that had outraged the conscience of the world. You were, however, carefully informed about the iniquities of the communist countries. If you read (between 1968 and 1980) the daily newspapers of my country, for instance, which had been confiscated by the military government, you would not find a word about the arrests of labor leaders, or of the murderous inflation. You would only read about what a happy and prosperous country Peru was and how much we Peruvians loved the military rulers. What happened with the press, television, radio, happened, too, most of the time, with the universities. The government persistently interfered, teachers and students considered subversive or hostile to the official system were expelled, and the whole curriculum was reorganized according to political considerations. As an indication of what extremes of absurdity this "cultural policy" could reach, you must remember, for instance, that during the military regime in Uruguay, the sociology departments were closed indefinitely because the social sciences were considered subversive. In academic institutions subject to this manipulation and censorship, it is improbable that contemporary political, social, and economic problems of the country could be described and discussed freely. Academic knowledge in many Latin American countries was, as with the press and the media, a victim of the deliberate turning away from what objectively was happening in society. This vacuum was filled by literature.

This is not a modern phenomenon. Even during the colonial period, though more especially since Independence—in which intellectuals and writers played an important role—all over Latin America, novels, poems, and plays were (as Stendhal once said he wanted the novel to be) the mirrors in which Latin Americans could truly see their faces and examine their sufferings. What was, for political reasons, repressed or distorted in the press and in the schools and universities, all the evils that were buried by the military and economic elite that ruled the countries, the evils that were never mentioned in the speeches of the politicians, nor taught in the lecture halls, nor criticized in the congresses, nor discussed in magazines, found a vehicle of expression in literature.

So something curious and paradoxical occurred. The realm of imagination became in Latin America the kingdom of objective reality; fiction was a substitute for social science; our best teachers about reality were the dreamers, the literary artists. And this is true not only for our great essayists—Domingo Faustino Sarmiento, José Martí, Manuel González Prada, José Enrique Rodó, José Vasconcelos, José Carlos Mariátegui, Octavio Paz—whose books are indispensable to us for a thorough comprehension of the historical and social reality of their respective countries, it is also valid for the writers who only practiced the creative literary genres of narration, poetry, and theatre. We can say without exaggeration that the most representative and genuine description of the real problems of Latin America during the nineteenth century is to be found in literature, and that it was in the verses of the poets or the plots of the narrators that, for the first time, the social evils of Latin America were denounced.

We have a very illustrative case with what it is called *indigenismo*, the literary current that, from the middle of the nineteenth century until the first decades of our century, had the Indian peasant of the Andes and his problems as the main subject. The writers in this movement were the first to describe the terrible conditions in which the Indians were still living three centuries after the Spanish Conquest, the impunity with which they were abused and exploited by the land proprietors—the *latifundistas* (estate owners), the *gamonales* (bosses)—the men who sometimes owned land as big as a European country, where they were absolute kings who treated their Indians worse, and sold them cheaper, than their cattle. The first "indigenist" writer was a woman, Clorinda Matto de Turner, an energetic and enthusiastic reader of the French novelist Emile Zola and positivist philosophers. Her novel *Aves sin nido* (*Birds without a Nest*) opened a road of social commitment to the problems and aspects of Indian life that Latin American writers would follow, examining in detail and from all angles, denouncing injustices, and praising and rediscovering the values and traditions of an Indian culture that, until then, at once incredibly and ominously, had been systematically ignored by the official culture. There is no way to research and analyze the rural history of the continent and understand the tragic destiny of the inhabitants of the Andes since it ceased to be a colony if you do not go through their books. They constitute the best—and sometimes the only—testimony of this aspect of our reality.

Am I saying with this, that because of the author's moral and social commitment, this literature is good literature, that because of their generous and courageous goals of breaking the silence about the real problems of society and of contributing towards the solution of these problems, that this literature is an artistic accomplishment? Not at all. What actually happened in many cases was the contrary. The pessimistic dictum of André Gide—who said once that with good sentiments you have bad literature—can be, alas, true. The "indigenist" literature is very important from a historical and social point of view, but only in exceptional cases is it of artistic importance. These novels or poems written, in general, very quickly, impelled by the present situation, with militant passion, obsessed with the idea of denouncing a social evil, of correcting a wrong, lack most of what is essential in a work of art: richness of expression, technical originality. Because of their didactic intentions, they became simplistic and superficial; because of their political partisanship they are sometimes demagogic and melodramatic; and because of their nationalist or regionalist scope, they can be very provincial and quaint. We can say that many of these writers, in order to serve better moral and social needs, sacrificed their vocation at the altar of politics. Instead of artists, they chose to be moralists, reformers, politicians, revolutionaries.

You can judge from your own particular system of values if this sacrifice is right or wrong, if the immolation of art for social and political aims is worthwhile or not. I am not dealing now with this problem. What I am trying to explain is how the particular circumstances of Latin American life have traditionally been orienting literature in this direction and how this has created for writers a very special situation. In one sense people—the real or potential readers of the writer—are used to considering literature as something intimately associated with living and social problems, the activity through which all that is repressed or disfigured in society will be named, described, and criticized. They expect novels, poems, and plays to counterbalance the policy of disguising and deforming reality, which is current in the media and official culture, and to keep alive the hope and spirit of change and revolt among the victims of that policy. In another sense this confers on the writer, as a citizen, a kind of moral and spiritual leadership, and he must try, during his life as a writer, to act according to this image of this role that he is expected to play. Of course he can reject it and refuse this task that society wants to impose on him and, declaring that he does not want to be either a politician or a moralist, or a sociologist, only an artist, seclude himself in this personal dream. But this will be considered (and, in a way, it is) a political, a moral, and a social choice. He will be considered by his real and potential readers as a deserter and traitor. And his poems, novels, and plays will be endangered. To be an artist, only an artist, can become, in this context, a kind of moral crime, a political sin. All our literature is marked by this fact and, if this is not taken into consideration, you cannot fully understand all the differences that exist between it and other literatures of the world.

No writer in Latin America is unaware of the pressure that is put on him, pushing him to a social commitment. Some accept this because this external impulse coincides with their innermost feelings and personal convictions. These cases are, surely, the happy ones. The coincidence between the individual choice of the writer and the idea of his vocation that society has, permits the novelist, poet, or playwright to create freely, without any pangs of conscience, knowing that he is supported and approved by his contemporaries. It is interesting to note that many Latin American men and women whose writing started out as totally uncommitted, indifferent, or even hostile to social problems and politics, later, sometimes gradually, sometimes abruptly, oriented their writings in this direction. The reason for this change could be, of course, that they adopted new attitudes, acknowledging the terrible social problems of our countries, an intellectual discovery of the evils of society and the moral decision to fight them. But we cannot dismiss as impossible that (consciously or unconsciously) the psychological and practical troubles it means for a writer to resist had a role in this change, along with the social pressure for political commitment, with the psychological and practical advantages that brought him to act and to write as society expects him to.

All this has given Latin American literature peculiar features. Social and political problems constitute a central subject for it, and they are present everywhere, even in the works in which, because of their theme and form, one would never expect to find them.

Take the case, for example, of the "literature of fantasy" as opposed to "realist literature." This kind of literature, whose raw material is subjective fantasy, does not reflect, usually, the mechanisms of economic injustice in society, nor the problems faced by urban and rural workers that make up the objective facts of reality, but—as in Edgar Allan Poe or Villiers de L'Isle-Adam—this literature builds a new reality, essentially different from "objective reality," out of the most intimate obsessions of writers. But in Latin America (mostly in modern times but also in the past) fantastic literature also has its roots in objective reality and is a vehicle for exposing social and political evils. So, fantastic literature becomes, in this way, symbolistic literature in which, disguised with the prestigious clothes of dreams and unreal beings and facts, we recognize the characters and problems of contemporary life. We have many examples among contemporary Latin American writers of this "realistic" utilization of unreality. The Venezuelan Salvador Garmendia has described, in short stories and novels of nightmarish obsessions and impossible deeds, the cruelty and violence of the streets of Caracas and the frustrations and sordid myth of the lower middle classes of that city. In the only novel of the Mexican Juan Rulfo, *Pedro Páramo*—all of whose characters, the reader discovers in the middle of the book, are dead—fantasy and magic are not procedures to escape social reality; on the contrary, they are simply other means to represent the poverty and sadness of life for the peasants of a small Jalisco village. Another interesting case is Julio Cortázar. In his first novels and short stories we enter a *fantastic* world, which is very mischievous because it is ontologically different from the world that we know by reason and experience, but has, at the first approach, all the appearances—features—of real life.

In this world social problems and political statements do not exist, they are aspects of human experience that are omitted. But in his last books, and principally in his novel *Libro de Manuel* (*A Manual for Manuel*), politics and social problems have a place as important as pure fantasy. The "fantastic" element is merged, in this fiction, with statements and motifs that deal with underground militancy, terrorism, revolutions, and dictatorship.

What happens with prose happens also with poetry, and, as among novelists, you find this necessity for social commitment in all kinds of poets, even in those who, because of the nature of their themes, you would expect not to be excessively concerned with militancy.

It is worth noting, too, that the political commitment of writers and literature in Latin America is a result not only of the social abuse and economic exploitation of large sectors of the population by small minorities and brutal military dictatorships. There are also cultural reasons for this commitment, exigencies that the writer himself sees grow and take root in his conscience during and because of his artistic development. To be a writer, to discover this vocation and to choose to practice it pushes you inevitably, in Latin America, to discover all the handicaps and miseries of underdevelopment. Iniquities, injustice, exploitation, discrimination, abuse are not only the burden of peasants, workers, employees, minorities. They are also social obstacles for the development of a cultural life. How can literature exist in a society where the rate of illiteracy reaches 50 or 60 percent? How can literature exist in countries where there are no publishing houses, where there are no literary publications, where if you want to publish a book you must finance it yourself? How can a cultural and literary life develop in a society where the material conditions of life—lack of education, subsistence wages, etc.—establish a kind of cultural apartheid, that is, impede the majority of the inhabitants from buying and reading books? And if, besides all that, the political authorities have established a rigid censorship in the press, in the media, and in the universities, that is, in those places through which literature would normally find encouragement and an audience, how could the Latin American writer remain indifferent to social and political problems? In the practice itself of his art—in the obstacles that he finds for this practice—the Latin American writer has found reasons to become politically conscious and to submit to the pressures of social commitment.

We can say that there are some positive aspects in this kind of situation for literature. Because of that commitment, literature is forced to keep in touch with living reality, with the experiences of people, and it is prevented from becoming, as sometimes has happened in some modern societies, an esoteric and ritualistic experimentation in new forms of expression almost entirely disassociated from living experience. And because of social commitment, writers are obliged to be socially responsible for what they write and for what they do, because social pressure provides a firm barrier against the temptation of using words and imagination in order to play the game of moral irresponsibility, the game of the enfant terrible who (only at the level of words, of course) cheats, lies, exaggerates, and proposes the worst option.

But this situation has a lot of dangers, too. The function and the practice of literature can be entirely distorted if the creative writings are seen only (or even mainly) as the materialization of social and political aims. What is to be, then, the border line, the frontier, between history, sociology, and literature? Are we going to say that literature is only a degraded form (because its data are always dubious because of the place that fantasy has in it) of the social sciences? In fact, this is what literature is converted to if its most praised value is considered to be the testimony it offers of objective reality, if it is principally judged as a true record of what happens in society.

On the other hand, this opens the door of literature to all kinds of opportunistic attitudes and intellectual blackmail. How can I condemn, as an artistic failure, a novel that explicitly protests against the oppressors of the masses, without being considered an accomplice of the oppressor? How can I say that this poem that fulminates, in assonant verses, against the great corporations is a calamity without being considered an obsequious servant of imperialism? We know how this kind of simplistic approach to literature can be utilized by dishonest intellectuals and imposed easily on uneducated audiences.

The experience of social commitment can signify, also, the destruction of artistic vocations that because of the particular sensibility, experiences, and temperament of a writer, he is unable to accomplish in his writings and actions what society expects of him. The realm of sensibility, of human experience, and of imagination is wider than the realm of politics and social problems. A writer like Jorge Luis Borges has built a great literary work of art in which this kind of problem is entirely ignored: metaphysics, philosophy, fantasy, and literature are more important for him. (But he was unable to keep himself from answering the social call for commitment, and one is tempted to see in what were his incredible statements of right-wing conservatism, statements that scared sometimes even the conservatives, just a strategy of political sacrilege in order not to be disturbed once and for all in his writings.) And many writers are not really prepared to deal with political and social problems. These are the unhappy cases. If they prefer their intimate call and produce uncommitted work, they will have to face all kinds of misunderstanding and rejection. Incomprehension and hostility will be their constant reward. If they submit to social pressure and try to write about social and political themes, it is quite probable that they will fail as writers, that they will frustrate themselves as artists for not having acted as their feelings prompted them to do.

I think that José María Arguedas experienced this terrible dilemma, and that all his life and work bears the trace of it. He was born in the Andes and, in spite of being the son of a lawyer, he was raised among the Indian peasants and, until his adolescence, was—in the language he spoke and in his vision of the world—an Indian. Later, he was recaptured by his family and he became a middle class Spanish-speaking Peruvian white. He lived always torn between these two different cultures and societies. And literature meant for him, in his first books, *Agua* (Water), *Yawar Fiesta*, *Los ríos profundos* (*Deep Rivers*), a melancholic escape to the days and places of his childhood, the world of the little Indian villages—San Juan de Lucanas Puquio—or towns of the Andes—Abancay—whose landscapes and customs he described in a tender and poetic prose. But, later, he felt obliged to renounce this kind of lyric image to fulfill the social responsibilities that everybody expected of him. And he wrote a very ambitious book, *Todas las sangres* (All the blood), in which he tried, escaping from himself, to describe the social and political problems of his country. The novel is a total failure; the vision is simplistic, even a caricature. We do not find any of the great literary virtues that made his previous books genuine works of art. The book is the classic failure of an artistic talent due to the self-imposition of social commitment. The other books of Arguedas oscillate between those two sides of his personality, and it is probable that all this played a part in his suicide.

When he pressed the trigger of the gun, in the University of La Molina, on the second day of December of 1969, José María Arguedas was, too, in a way, showing how difficult and daring it can be to be a writer in Latin America.

I have been using, in this paper, the past tense. Why? Well, things have been improving politically—at least in Latin America. In the last several years, almost all Latin American countries have replaced authoritarian and military regimes by civilian and elected governments. With the exception of Peru and Haiti, the rest of the continent can be called "democratic" and free, although there are, of course, different levels of commitments towards freedom and participation in these new regimes. But you can assume, I believe, without excessive optimism, that there is a new political enthusiasm in Latin Americans towards the Western liberal and democratic system which, in the past, was despised and rejected by the Right and the Left. If this process continues, this will have, for sure, an effect on literature, and writers will gradually lose incentives and pressures to commit themselves to political and social causes. Is this prospect something to celebrate or to deplore? I have mixed feelings about it.

Panel Discussion

Panelists: William H. Gass, Janet Majerus,
Margaret Sayers Peden, Randolph Pope, Luisa Valenzuela

Luisa Valenzuela: I think Mario does have mixed feelings. He spoke about political commitment as something imposed from the outside, by the demands of the society. I don't think any real writer would feel that obligation. Writers such as Mario Vargas Llosa have written from the core of their feelings and have always, in some way or other, knowingly or unknowingly, been committed to the social fabric of their own country. I cannot say as he did that the first of Cortázar's books were not socially oriented. *Los premios* (*The Winners*) was a very sociological book. It's not a good novel, but it is very sociologically oriented. It was a criticism about the division of classes. Also the novel of his that was published after his death, *The Exam*, was a very critical view of what Buenos Aires became later, a place completely obsessed by the oppression of people.

My experience is very different. I don't come from a country that is as illiterate; the readership in Argentina is much larger. We had (but don't anymore) the best publishing houses in Latin America. I found myself writing in some sort of "committed" way not because I felt I would sell better; on the contrary, I sold much less. People were scared of me in Argentina; I lost readership. But I had to say what I felt I had to say. In my country, people didn't want to hear what was going on, what is *still* going on in certain places. It is very hard for the writer to tell about the horrors, because you do not want to face the brutality of government, the terrorism, the torture that was going on in our countries. You can put yourself at risk by writing about that. And you know that people won't want to listen to that; people want the writer to make easy denunciations. The real writing exposes the dark side that is in every one of us, and which is very important. The mission of the writer is not to do what is expected; it is what we need to do in spite of ourselves.

Randolph Pope: When I was seventeen or eighteen, there was a little book that circulated among us that had been published in Cuba. It was one of the texts we had to discuss because it demanded a decision from us. It was the book with a rather furious dialogue that had taken place between Oscar Collazos, Julio Cortázar, and Mario Vargas Llosa. Mario Vargas Llosa was arguing for writing a novel that was not local, a novel that wouldn't speak only about the problems that were Latin American problems, a novel that could be read in St. Louis, Missouri, and could generate a symposium. Collazos was saying that if we did that, something would be left behind. José María Arguedas, for example, told of the Indians in a literature that was different. He tried to express the voice of the laborers and the Indians in the different parts of Peru. His novel *El zorro de arriba y el zorro de abajo* (The top fox and the bottom fox), one of his last, is extremely complex, and failed, but it is a very daring experiment. So I see Mario's paper as a form of reconciliation, as a continuation of that dialogue that was important to all of us so long ago.

My question is this: Have novelists been the chroniclers of our continent? I think our story has never been told, because we were mostly middle-class white men, well-educated, and couldn't quite grasp what was going on at the roots of Latin America. This has been the case in Spain where intellectuals have discovered they were left behind by the country itself. I question this assumption that novelists have actually been the historians of Latin America. I think it's a continent that has not had its history written yet and is still open for future novels, so maybe we could agree that novelists have been close to being historians—but not quite.

Mario Vargas Llosa: I certainly think that many problems are left behind, even when you have already reached committed literature. What I pointed out was the case of these particular social and political problems that traditionally were not expressed and criticized outside of literature. Literature became the natural vehicle to express these kinds of problems and to describe the phenomenon of the big landowners, and the relationship between them and the peasants. It was because of literature that the essential problem for many countries in Latin America became an issue in our culture. We had an idea of Latin America that was completely stereotyped and imported. It was only through literature, and very late in the nineteenth century, that the physical world of Latin America was described, recognized, and understood in Latin America. This was not a political problem, but it was related to political problems. We also had a culture that was deeply alienated from the real world of Latin America. Literature was useful in overcoming this. I mentioned the case of the "indigenist" novel with its historical or sociological analysis of Latin America. From a literary point of view there were not many real achievements. Writers like Juan Rulfo and José María Arguedas are the exceptions.

Margaret Sayers Peden: We keep coming back to Neruda. I think of his Nobel Prize acceptance speech in which he said that the role of the Latin American writer is to fill the empty spaces, to give things names. I always assumed he meant the things beyond the geographical, the reality of Latin America. I want to bring Bill Gass into the discussion.

William H. Gass: I see this problem as a Platonic one, involving three different regions of politics where the problems are, to my mind, remarkably similar. One is what I call the politics of the page, the words, the place where I'm most at home and where I have my most real experiences. On the page you have a political situation. You have every possible element of your prose and your project demanding to be in charge. There's alliteration wanting to be present, assonance, consonants, rhythm saying, "Hey, wait, don't forget the meter, you rhymed up here. Don't forget the parallel constructions," and then you have a symbol that's whining in the corner, several characters who need development, and so on. Each one wants to have it all his way, to be the ruler of the page. This is an internal struggle and can be called the arena of sincerity. Every once in awhile, of course, you will say to yourself, indicating a weakness or corruption, "Oh, I shouldn't write 'fuck' here, people don't like that." That's a sign of the external pressure, which we have been talking about. I think it is naive to have an optimistic view of writers' characters. We do risk begging the question about writers if we say, "Well, you know, if you're a *real* writer, then you don't do this or that, and you don't bend to external pressures and so on." Well, then there are very few real writers left. But here you are, on the page, presuming you are responding to real issues, that there is a rhetorical structure, it does demand its weight, and has its voice. In an ideal republic, you would be able to satisfy all of these demands with the great stroke of your next line. That would be called the grace of greatness. And everything that was yelling and howling would be happy.

That's very similar to what's going on in another realm: the politics of the person, the interior motives of the writing self, for the writer is an interiorization of a tremendous number of impulses to write. You'd better have a lot of them because you need every bit of energy you have to get the task done. I've always envied poets, because they only have to be inspired for ten minutes or so at a time. If you're writing a novel you may have to drag that inspiration through several marriages and political revolutions. So you have to marshal every bit of your energy because all these impulses will want to take over—all the things that you wanted to say about your miserable childhood (as if no one else had ever suffered before), all the things that you hated about your teachers, your first wife, the politics of the country, the bad deans, so on and so forth. Each one of these things, including the better part of your character (always the weaker voice), and then all of the meanness, the envy, the spite, the scoring, rendering of accounts, and so on—are dangerous to banish. I think writing out of hate is much better than writing out of love, because hate is genuine.

The third politics, which we've been talking about, is the politics of public life. There are all these interests wanting the ball, most of them having a genuine right and value, which somehow has to be realized, integrated, harmonized, and so on. For the writer what is crucial is the aesthetic and formal impulse (here, of course the Platonic gets in and in full cry): it is the ruler. Your book will fail if you do not ultimately dominate it, however much you may have a cause and however much you may be afflicted with belief. Belief is an affliction, from my point of view, the fewer of which one has the better. I love Francis Herbert Bradley's remark that beliefs are like stinking fish, and should be held lightly by the tail at arms length, ready to drop at a moment's notice. What makes you an artist is the management of those impulses and the placement of them under the proper formal rigor. Then you can have it all: a politics in which you can reveal to the world all kinds of so-called truths, you can believe you're saving society, saving yourself, getting even with your mother-in-law, and so on. Those things will have ruined you unless you have kept that ultimate control. That's in, I think, all three politics.

Audience Member (Peruvian poet Miguel Angel Zapata): This discussion has focused on the history of literature in Latin America. What is going to happen to writing in Peru when the present situation is overcome? What will happen to writing in the future?

Mario Vargas Llosa: What is happening in Latin America is not, unfortunately, what is happening in Peru, where we have technically a dictatorship. (Even if this dictatorship has some popular support, it is still a dictatorship.) We still have to overcome this old obstacle to real progress. We can say that in Latin America there is political progress, in the sense that the democratic system is taking root, not only because we have civilian governments and pluralistic societies, but because for the first time there is popular support for the system. If this keeps on and we don't go backwards, I imagine that what would happen with Latin American literature would be something similar to what happened in Spain. During the 1960s and 1970s, under the pressure of the Franco regime, literature was very political. Social problems were predominant for writers and for intellectuals in general. Then Spain had this transition towards democracy, an extraordinary experience for the peaceful way in which it was done. Now you don't really recognize the preoccupations, interests, the goals of writers, intellectuals, and artists in Spain compared with twenty years ago. Now political commitment for the writer is very rare. Writers and intellectuals in Spain are mostly indifferent to political matters, they even possess cynical attitudes. Most writers now are much more secluded in their own writing as in the other "advanced" societies. They are indifferent or perhaps deeply assured that these problems can find a solution through the mechanisms of the new society. If the democratic process consolidates in Latin America perhaps something similar will happen for literature. I don't know if this will be good or bad, because the tremendous pressures in Latin America and the terrible situation in economic, political, and social terms has had at least one very positive result: it has produced the ambitious literature that these kinds of societies in crisis historically have been able to produce. A stable society doesn't usually produce great literature. Probably if Latin America improves politically and becomes a modern continent then our literature would be less crazy, less anarchic, less ambitious, and more predictable.

Luisa Valenzuela: I wouldn't want a literature that is not in some way committed, even though I don't believe in committed literature as such. People want to forget; they think that if they forget, then they will be able to move on. But we will not be able to move on if we don't know the past. Besides, our democracies are not that good. They are full of corruption and horrible management by the governments. Perhaps literature needn't focus on these problems directly. Now that we have freedom of expression, newspapers are doing that very well for us. We must try to say what we don't know, to keep on writing that history that was never completely written. Because it has always to be written. If being in a safe world would mean to forego writing I would rather be in a safe world, but of course that is impossible. There is no way that the world will not be full of victims on whose side writers will always be, one way or the other.

Randolph Pope: Look at other examples of what has happened in Chile and in Spain after restoring democracy. A few unpredictable things have taken place. One of them has to do with the feminist, gay, and lesbian literature. Some books such as *The Same Sea As Every Summer* by Esther Tusquets have become instant classics. What happens with democracy is that many other forms of repression become visible and writers begin to address these issues.

Janet Majerus: I think the ideas for change come not from the fiction side but from the nonfiction side. We are becoming creatures of television and radio much more so than of books and newspapers. We look back and we think, "Oh, so and so wrote this book. That was the start of the movement," but it tends more to come out of the masses, and then the intelligentsia pick up on it and magnify it.

Randolph Pope: I feel strongly that books do influence people and societies. It's where ideas and images circulate. Certainly the Bible has transformed people, so has *Mein Kampf*; the journals of Che Guevara transformed people when I was a university student; and so did Simone de Beauvoir. They have changed other things: departments, canons, and our lives.

Audience Member (Playwright Joan Lipkin): You were talking earlier about the way literature can address certain kinds of oppression. Literature seeks to uncover discrimination, such as with gay and lesbian literature, and there will always be another level to which literature can aspire. My question is if there are always going to be problems to resolve in literature, must we always move to these higher levels? If so, it seems that I can't write a book in which the main character is not politically correct because somehow this is going to reflect on my politics and on society.

Margaret Sayers Peden: I think that was touched upon briefly in Mario's comments about intellectual blackmail.

William H. Gass: I don't think that a writer should get anywhere near an ideology that starts telling him or her what to think or do. That's external pressure to be resisted. The writer may be interested in rendering an individual character in a certain way, but there must be absolute freedom. You have to justify every action you make on the page in terms of the book itself. Anything else is artistic inter-ference, and I'm absolutely opposed to it.

Randolph Pope: One thing that impressed me greatly about Vargas Llosa's novel *The Green House* when I read it for the first time, was that the Indians were not likable. Before this, Indians were always handsome and good, and expressed themselves beautifully. Mario very courageously broke a tradition. Was that something you were thinking about while writing *La casa verde,* that you had this tradi-tion to fight against? Were you worried that some people would say that your Indians were not graceful enough?

Mario Vargas Llosa: That was a very interesting problem for me. One of the stories from *La casa verde* is based on something that ac-tually happened in the Amazon region, something I discovered on a journey there. I think it was my first experience of seeing the extreme barbarism that the exploitation of Indians reached in Peru. I wanted to put in the novel what was the real incident that inspired the episode in the novel and I couldn't. It was totally impossible for me to invent this terrible experience from the perspective of a very primitive man from a very small tribe in the Amazon. I felt that there was no power of persuasion in this episode. Finally I resigned myself to broadening the episode and to tell it not from the point of view of the protago-nist, the Indian himself, but from the perspective of people whom I could invent more easily. That was one of my first lessons about the impossibility of being totally truthful when you write a fiction. Fic-tion pushes you inevitably to distort and to transform the real world. That is one reason why the literary testimony, the testimony that cre-ated texts give about the real world, should be always taken with great suspicion.

Audience Member: I'd like to ask Mr. Vargas Llosa if he experiences the writing process as Mr. Gass explained it, as a process of overcom-ing the impulses and getting at the story?

Mario Vargas Llosa: I should make a comment on my own paper. What I have tried to describe is not the creative process from the perspective of a creative writer. I have mentioned only one aspect of the effect that social and cultural pressure can have on a literary work. I think the creative process is an individual one in which there is inevitably an interaction of conscious and unconscious elements. I think in most cases the presence of these two sides of human personality are such that it's very difficult for the writer, the creator himself, to have a clear view of the whole. I am talking, of course, of my personal experience.

I have always tried to be very lucid when I write a novel. I try to organize the story, the characters, the structure, but what I am expecting is to have all of these rational preparations be, in any given moment, destroyed by spontaneous impulses, instincts, and obsessions, which come from a very deep part of my personality. I know this has happened when I discover surprises within my own stories. There are some forces there I have to respect. There are elements I was not entirely conscious of putting in, and for me this is what is exciting in the creative process: to discover that you don't write a novel only with reason, with ideas; a novel is something that requires your total participation.

That is why, when a writer imposes on himself a subject, a theme for rational reasons, what he's doing is suppressing the participation of this obscure side of his personality which in most cases is the real motor of inspiration, of creation. I think the process is something very mysterious in which, even if you are an intellectual writer, you open many doors and put into your writing something that comes from the whole of your personality. For that reason I can't agree more with Bill when he says that hate is more functional for the creative process than love. You don't write with only positive feelings. You write also with negative feelings. You write because you hate. You write because you want to take revenge against the world, a world you don't accept. Sometimes you take revenge because you don't know why you don't accept the world. And you try to understand all of this. When you are able to put all of this at the service of the creative process there are more chances to accomplish an original and lasting work of art.

Audience Member (Professor William Matheson): I'd like to agree heartily with Bill Gass in his support of art for art's sake, but I'm wondering if we're going to take up the problem of what a work of art is? Is it what it was thirty years ago? What is the novel? What is commitment? What is style? And does anybody care?

William H. Gass: I agree it's changing and changing enormously. Previously, in our culture, values were determined by the church and then the state, but now they are governed by the marketplace. Commerce is interested in consumption, in things wearing out, in turnover. It's not interested in trying to sell one product everywhere, but in many places. This makes for a superficial pluralism, and the notion of a universal work is no longer necessary. If you can sell a lot of different products in different parts of the world, what does it matter to your profit line? It's a more advantageous idea now—to support a plurality of tastes, types, and times. So I think that you're quite right. Those old arty notions started to go in the 1960s. I remember my students saying, "Well, why write a poem that lives and lives? Just replace the old model with a newer one."

Audience Member: I have a question for Mario Vargas Llosa. It seems that there are many of the same problems and conflicts in Eastern Europe as in Latin America. For example, Vaclav Havel's presidency seems to have been influenced by the fact that he was a writer. What happens when a writer enters politics? If you had become president, would your presidency have been influenced by your having been a writer, and if so, how?

Mario Vargas Llosa: I cannot disassociate myself of my writings, so if I would have been president of Peru, I would have been the same person: a writer who has all these preoccupations. But certainly, I wouldn't have acted as president as I act when I write a novel. I think in politics it is very important to keep in the rational realm and to repress obsessions, instincts, passions. I think this is one of the reasons we are in bad shape in countries like mine, because reason has been overcome in politics by passion. I am convinced that politics should be rational, made out of ideas, and that we must not permit irrationality to take over. With literature, I think exactly the opposite. I think we must open the door to the demons of our souls. Literature is the ideal way to express and get rid of all these very nasty parts of our personality. The demons are there and are very dangerous if we permit them to act freely in politics. This has been true particularly in Peru in the last ten years. But we cannot deny the existence of the demons, so we must try to give them some sort of citizenship. I think art is the ideal way with which to open the door of the city to the demons and to keep them tamed. When I write a novel, I am very pleased with my demons, and I try to call them, and I know they help me a lot as a writer. That, I think, should be the border between art and politics.

The first part of your question was about Vaclav Havel. I think Havel is the successful case of a writer involved in politics. I think what he did for his country was great, and the way he did it was very much influenced by the fact that he was a writer. I think what he brought to politics in Czechoslovakia is something that a writer or an artist can offer: a moral perspective, more important than the purely political, and a new discourse—a discourse without the stereotypes and the wooden language that is the norm in the political discourse. Vaclav Havel was the extraordinary case of the politician whose speeches you could read because they were full of ideas, and there was something authentic there. He proved to the people that politics is not only about intrigue, maneuvering, and sordid appetites, but also about something in which idealism, ideas, creativity, and authenticity can take place, and that these can produce positive changes in society. I think it's a positive example of how not all writers are so ineffective in politics, as I am myself, for example.

Margaret Sayers Peden: As we have a successful politician on our panel who is a novelist, perhaps we should have a word from Janet.

Janet Majerus: Being head of a city of 40,000 is not exactly like heading up a country. But I do have to agree that if you are a writer and then are elected to office, you certainly can't behave as you did when you were a writer. You do have to become politically correct. However, I think there is a major advantage in having a writing background and being in politics. I will pick up on the theme of the demons. You can recognize the demons in the other people. You can often disarm them because your powers of observation are more highly developed. I do think it is an advantage, but it certainly plays havoc with your writing. If you become a politician—and I do think you were fortunate that you didn't—it pretty well squelches your creative writing, and it panics all the people around you because they think you're secretly writing the novel that is going to expose them to the world.

Luisa Valenzuela: I am interested in this dichotomy that Mario was pointing to with the writer and the demons. If you repress your own demons, you will try to repress the demons of others. You must not repress them, but understand and transform them. One must acknowledge the good that can be derived from their evil and how you can transform them into something positive. What the politicians are trying to do is to deny the dark aspect of the society, and we are trying to see it in its face, to name it, and then to exorcise it in some way or another.

William H. Gass: Mario, you disturbed me a little bit with what sounded awfully Aristotelian, this idea of the catharsis of bad emotions. Aristotle knew exactly why he wanted to do that, so the state would stay on an even keel. That will work fine if the state is ideal, but then you go to the theatre and have this catharsis of evil feelings; they are discharged safely in a safe place, and you don't rock the boat. The problem is that I don't know a boat that shouldn't sink.

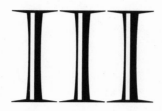

The Writer under a Politics

4 Trying to Breathe

Luisa Valenzuela

■ Yesterday I was reminded by Bill Gass about a quote by F. H. Bradley about how beliefs are actually stinking fish that ought to be held at arm's length. In turn I was reminded of the *hadith*, and those things attributed to the prophet Mohammed, who said: "Faith is a glowing ember in the believer's palm." It was Luisa Valenzuela, whom I have the pleasure to introduce, who said in *The Lizard's Tail*: "I, Luisa Valenzuela, swear by these writings that I will try to do something about all this." Please welcome Luisa Valenzuela.

ANTON SHAMMAS, *Moderator*

Trying to Breathe

To say "the writer under a politics" is for me just like saying the writer alive, or out in the open, under the clouds, in the eye of the storm if necessary. Is there anywhere else to be, anyway?

Yes, on a desert island.

Yes, in an ivory tower.

The latter location, dated as it sounds, has been simply replaced by the crystal skyscraper, just as mythical and isolating.

No writer walking down these god-forsaken streets can be immune to the political fabric that surrounds her like a muggy spider web. The world breathes politics, eats politics, defecates politics. The trick is to avoid writing directly about politics while not losing contact, still being profoundly politically aware. It involves a kind of Zen and the art of archery of language: you shoot the arrow of language without burdening it with a message, and if it is a good arrow, if the shot is correctly aimed, it will hit its political mark, a mark that even the writer might not be aware of when she starts to shoot, when she begins to write. This is my favorite way of approaching a text: there is a perception, a feeling, a phrase, and at that very frail point I jump blindly into the work as into a swimming pool, without knowing how much water there might be. Often I bang my head against the bottom, there is nothing to be said, or at least no metaphor or association to unveil, nothing appears or is hinted at beyond my words.

I write to understand, to discover, and with a sense of adventure. Otherwise the writing might fall flat and everything has to go to the wastepaper basket, not the worst of places, to be honest—much more frightening is the purgatory of overstatement and literalness.

When things are working well, I allow language to lead me by the nose and take me to the most—I hope—unexpected places. In the tricky subject of politics, language knows so much more than I do that it can sometimes become unbearable.

The act of writing requires a crossing of boundaries, a breaking of barriers, and not only the external barriers of commercial demands or official censorship so blatant under a dictatorship; the worst obstacle may be that absconded form of self-censorship that Freudians call negation. Once the feat of trespassing is performed, not without pain, words will start living on their own and the turn of a phrase might allow us to catch a glimpse of the truth. Some decoding will take place, some deciphering. Which is as far as we aspire to go. For there is one thing a writer who is politically aware and concerned can do and often does: she can undermine certainty, thus combating those—people in power and in organized religions—who believe themselves to be owners of the Truth.

Writers are not necessarily excluded from this threatening category nor are literary critics. Very different would have been the destiny of deconstructionism in the United States had it not been for Paul de Man who, probably because of a need to deconstruct his own dark past, turned a rich theory into a boring, stifling lens through which to distort a text. Self-service is not what language is alive for. There is only one position with regard to language, from a literary point of view, and that is to allow it to use you.

Years ago I wrote a text on this somewhat abstract subject. I would like to read it here in an attempt to clarify what I am trying to convey. The title is, to say the least, tongue in cheek:

A Little Manifesto

We tend to forget that behind every writer there is a dormant human being, ready to jump at the smallest provocation of the world around us and/or at the slightest tickle of the quill. If for Borges, man (meaning the human being) is a literary animal, one can also say that the human being is a political animal. And it is not a question of a clear or easy option, but rather of a conflictive duality with which we must learn to coexist. The literary animal in each writer requires inner tranquillity and some inclination or ability to withdraw from external preoccupations, while the political animal doesn't allow the writer to do that, every so often awakening us from our daydream with a treasonous clawing. The world goes on and we are part of the world, and if there is a change of factions or if there is a war somewhere, we know that, for better or worse, matters will no longer be the same and neither will we be the same.

Should we write for or against these topics? Perhaps in some newspaper article, a territory where opinions have a direct value. Because literature is something else, literature is the site of the crosswaters—the murky and the clear ones—where nothing is exactly in its place because there is no precise place. We have to invent it each time.

If we believe we have an answer to the world's problems, it befits us to be politicians and attempt to solve them with the power politics provides us. Literature doesn't pretend to solve anything. It disturbs and stirs ideas, keeping them from becoming stale. But it is precisely at these crosswaters where it becomes necessary to have a lucid ideology as a base from which problems may be focused on, exploring new options.

I don't believe writers are or should be judges; neither should we pretend to be the blind, beautiful Justice. We are simply witnesses with our antennae alert, witnesses to our external and internal realities, intertwined as they always are. For me, the literary act neither centers on the marionette nor on the hand which moves it. The literary act hopes to capture the elusive threads which go from one to the other. And trying to see these threads forces us to squint. The clarity of our vision will be greater the less we pretend to impose a preconceived image and the more we alert ourselves to terror.

Writing is a game of constant questioning and it is a dangerous one, and not because we might be fighting against some kind of censorship but rather because we can never permit ourselves the comfortable solid ground of absolute certainty, where dwell those who have killed the political animal or the literary animal inherent in themselves and so are called, respectively, literati or politicians.

Long before I even dreamed of writing, of becoming a writer, I was faced with the false idea that there was an option, a dichotomy, a pair of mutually excluding opposites. It was during the Jorge Luis Borges/Ernesto Sábato debate, very intense in the literary Buenos Aires of the early 1950s, when the intelligentsia banded together as a protection against Juan Perón's persecution. Both great writers would frequent my maternal home, not necessarily at the same time, and the ongoing discussion seemed to be a matter of life or death. Should we be for Borges's "art for art's sake" or for Sábato's "committed" literature? I would listen attentively to both arguments and believe more in art for art's sake. It sounded better to a very young, adolescent ear, nobler in that you were not imposing your ideology on others, or that foul word for many writers: your *message*.

The never-ending debate took place in secret, behind closed doors and windows—not a breath of fresh air to mitigate the heat of the argument—for those were times of denunciations and fear. The matter under discussion was the purity of literature, but the overall feeling was that of a political meeting. Curiously enough, none of the writers present were focusing on politics in their fiction or their poetry. We may surmise that the same closed doors and windows that allowed them to speak without being heard by the outside world also separated them from the sound, the fury, the rumors, the bangs, clashes, and screams from the outside. It is true that what the writers I knew feared most then was claustrophobia in the police van, not torture and slow death as some of our colleagues would experience twenty years later.

Argentine letters, though, did not suffer because of the political naiveté of many of its important authors. After all, Borges, Adolfo

Bioy Casares, Silvina Ocampo, Mujica Lainez, and others were writing their masterpieces at the time.

As in all of Latin America, we had to wait for the Cuban Revolution and the politicized 1960s to change our perception, and at some point we realized that there is no dichotomy between the old concept of art for art's sake and a political commitment in art. This merging became the essence of the new Latin American novel; only now the power structures insist on imposing that false opposition, the old Manichaeism. One of the most important tasks of the writer is to combat Manichaeism of all kinds.

The idea of setting tasks for a writer is abominable, but I'll confess to a few I seem to set for myself. The first and obvious one is to acknowledge contradictions, to play with them, to pull them out in the open so as not to fall prey, for example, to our present president's discourse. I want to play with contradiction as a cat would with a mouse; I want to appropriate the toy, see how it works, stop it from playing with us.

In this respect I had a powerful experience while writing *The Lizard's Tail*. The question that set this novel rolling—for my usual point of departure is a question—was why we Argentines, who pretend to be so "European," were for so many years in the hands of a self-confessed sorcerer? The man was José López Rega, Isabel Perón's former minister of social welfare, creator of the Triple A, the Argentine Anti-Communist Alliance, the agency that initiated state terrorism in my country.

I started the novel without a clear idea of where it would lead me. Only one thing was certain: it wouldn't be written in the third person. I needed to give the protagonist a voice, otherwise I would become terribly critical, and I didn't want to write a judgmental novel. And suddenly this character came to life. The sorcerer spoke, and since his discourse is that of a messianic madman, he took over language and became powerful. And he was much more intelligent than I. He began to fool around with me and turn me around, to become the owner of the language. I even started experiencing sympathy for him. So I felt in some way threatened, and out of real need wrote the following paragraph:

> I, Luisa Valenzuela, swear by these writings that I will try to do something about all this, become involved as much as possible, plunge in head-first, aware of how little can be

done but with the desire to handle at least a small thread and assume responsibility for the story.

Which is what a writer probably intends to do all along, but since that other reality called fiction has its own inner pulse, I assumed responsibility then and there and some hundred pages later had to relinquish it, allowing the novel to go on without me, with myself as a very secondary character, as I don't believe the writer should be suffused in the text to that extent.

The function of the writer is that of a mirror, sometimes a distorting mirror with which to enhance and reveal. The function of the writer is that of antennae. A sounding board, let's say, for the discourse of power, which most often is perverse and fascinating. I try to deconstruct the discourse of power, to see through it in the hope of understanding the deep truth it usually unveils in spite of the speaker. As Jean Baudrillard in *The Transparency of Evil* states:

> Beneath the transparency of the consensus lies the opacity of the principle of evil—the tenacity, obsessiveness and irreducibility of the evil whose contrary energy is at work everywhere: in the malfunctioning of things, in viral attacks, in the acceleration of processes and in their wildly chaotic effects.

Writing, if anything, is a form of reading, of reading reality, opening the way for new associations and connections and insights that will distance us from dogma and official "truths." As language is the writer's only tool, we expect to make readers aware of its double edge, its possibilities, and its implicit danger. One way or another, we naturally point out the snares that may be set with simple everyday words and show how easily people can be oppressed by language. A political consciousness regarding language is crucial, for whether under a dictatorship or the most benign democracy, there will always be oppressors and oppressed; it is a never-ending battle and we should be alert and ready to fight it at all times.

For this reason above all I admire the women's movement, for having made us aware of the oppressive possibilities of language. Our perception of reality is colored by the words chosen to describe it. We become what others name us, so the torturer will call his victim an animal, a swine, an insect, or vermin; even a torturer might hesitate to meticulously destroy a fellow human being.

The battle against labels and libels has to be fought with every word. It is a battle against stagnation, a lateral battle, of course, which is why sometimes the ambiguities in a text can be more clarifying than the certitudes.

I, for one, try to open doors for readers and allow them to discover as much as I discover while writing, hoping they will discover more, much more. Language is a treasure chest, a conjuring act, a set of Russian *matryoshkas*. It can also be an act of courage, of passion, and a recognition of what we lack.

My country, Argentina, is a country of wishful thinkers (wishful *sinkers*, to use Cabrera Infante's accurate pun). Argentines are a brilliant people rich in imagination but in desperate need of immediate gratification. We are always waiting for the charismatic figure to come and pull us out of our troubles. We are hoping for a father, a savior who will produce a miracle. So Argentina had Juan Perón, and now Carlos Saúl Menem with his dubious promise of finding a place among the first world countries, thanks to economic stability, applauded by a majority that disregards the very high social cost, the all-pervasive corruption, the impoverishment of the masses. Certainly we are not the only ones to succumb to political daydreaming, but I am afraid that at least in this respect, we triumph-hungry Argentines are the champions. By only seeing what we want to see and not what is before our eyes, we will take the best road to disaster. "*No hay peor ciego que el que no quiere ver,*" we say: "There is no worse blind man than the one who doesn't want to see."

In order to avoid such a trap, the role of memory is crucial. How often do we fall prey to the same yearning? As Argentines, we have a long history of demanding immediate changes and heroes, a yearning that brought military coups and dictatorships, clandestine detention camps and torture, a history of horror that many insist we should forget. Books are good for this, and also the larger book, reality, if we know how to read it.

Our favorite blind man, for example, who for many of his last years saw not so much what he wanted to see but what the others, who were acting as his eyes, were telling him to see, Borges, changed his mind one day. There was a moment when the best writing about our country was being done in a daily newspaper. There were vignettes of the trials of the generals and those who were convicted of torture and who, alas, are now free. (They were freed by the present government.) At the time of those trials, everything was coming out, everything that the Argentines had been hiding from themselves, the truth that we couldn't deal with, the things that we didn't want to acknowledge. Somebody had the idea of inviting Borges to witness one of the trials. As he was going in, a journalist (only one or two could be present) asked him, "Do you think they should be forgiven? Do you think we should pardon the military?" He replied, "Yes, I think forgiveness is a great, humane tool, and we must use it. We must pardon even the guilty." When he came out later he was asked the same question, and he said, "No, if a tenth of what I have heard here today is true, there is no pardon possible." There was a pardon, as I said, but things were known finally.

At the same time, Ernesto Sábato, the eternal rival of Borges (as he himself declared), was working with the National Commission on the Disappeared. They gathered the testimonies from the trials and published *Nunca Más* (Never again), the book that everybody should have in their homes even if it is unreadable because it is so terrible and so hard. At that point the Manichaeism was over, the two opposites touched, Borges and Sábato were on the same side, the side of the victims, the only place a writer can be.

It is a question of memory. In my country there is always someone trying to erase something, when he is not trying to erase somebody from the face of the earth. Politicians in power want to start with a clean slate, a clean past even if that past doesn't concern them directly. Now, for example, we are officially told that everything that went on during the military dictatorship, officially called the Process of National Reconstruction, with its 30,000 victims, needs to be forgotten in order to move on. Forgotten and even forgiven to the point that our present president granted amnesty to the members of the military juntas who had been tried and found guilty.

Multiple elements are used here to erase memory: contradictions, promises, pieces of gossip interwoven in the news, anything that can act as a delusory device to stop people from delving into the truth. Beyond the killings that took place years ago, there seems to be a need for killing without even leaving the faintest memory of the victim. In such a situation, we all become victims because we are forced to tread the fine line between oblivion and negation, below which are numerous unmarked graves and a horror that could be repeated.

The government wanted us to forget, to look towards the future, to move in a straight line. But with history's cyclical nature, forgetting can be dangerous. This is why those heroines of Argentina, the Mothers of the Plaza de Mayo, refused the straight line towards oblivion and continued to circle and circle in front of the government building, demanding an explanation and punishment for the guilty.

It is the Mothers of Plaza de Mayo who today save us from the ignominy of erasure. They compel us to recall. They did us the favor not only of facing the initial horror but of allowing us to accept our past without feeling guilty for it.

Those who want us to keep silent and to forget proclaim the linearity, the straight line which is not a synonym of rectitude, just the opposite: it is a line of escape meant to leave everything behind.

The Mothers, confronted with the threat of denial and oblivion, imposed the circle. The reiteration. Their white kerchiefs were in contrast to the black inkblot with which the men in power want to cross out the past of terror. The government wanted the color of mourning, a canceling color. The Mothers wore white, the clarity of light, encompassing all colors. Light had to be cast on the crimes even at the cost of reopening the wounds, so many years later, for proper healing cannot come from superficial bandages. The white kerchiefs the Mothers wore were embroidered with the names of their "disappeared" sons and daughters, a constant reminder of the darkest aspects of humanity.

Those who coined the noun "disappeared" do not want that white color to last. It acts as a screen on which the history of our pain may be projected. Those who turned that adjective into a noun wanted, thanks to the magic of language, to attain precisely what it meant: to have their victims disappear from the face of the earth. Evaporated, eclipsed, vanished forever, not a trace left. The Mothers, with their courageous perseverance, sustain the miracle of life by demanding clarification. The example of the Mothers of Plaza de Mayo gave Argentina the courage to fight against injustice, to stand up and word the various complaints.

Remembrance is a necessity. It is to keep memory alive that I write, to acknowledge memory, in Carlos Fuentes's words, as a "shared responsibility." For there will always be somebody around to inquire why we must dig into the rubble. We will always be denounced by someone who, with reason or not, is upset by unconscious guilt. There will always be somebody who does not want to hear about the painful matters of our past. Why not simply bury it? they will demand. As if time and history were elements one could slice and separate, as if it were just like going to the store and asking for three yards. Please cut it right there because further back the piece is defective. Don't unroll it that much.

It is not an easy task to look into the mire of the human potential for cruelty. Nor is it easy to write about what one sees. I find the tools of black humor, hyperrealism, the grotesque, and the absurd to be very helpful: they allow us to break the barriers of internal censorship, of the fear and horror that usually blur the vision; they act as a kind of smoky lens allowing us to focus directly on what we actually don't want to see, what we desperately would like to forget.

I now know it was to preserve my own memory that I left Argentina in January 1979, and it was to keep memory alive that I returned there ten years later.

In the late 1970s, gone were the times when state violence was out in the open and we could fight back one way or another, or at least sit in cafés, in the general atmosphere of paranoia and write stories about it, as I had done when completing the collection *Strange Things Happen Here*. After the military coup of 1976, during the peak of the dictatorship, I wrote *Cambio de armas* (*Other Weapons*), a novella about a tortured woman, which I felt I couldn't show even to my best friends. To ignore or pretend to ignore what was going on under the deceptively calm surface of the city seemed—and in some instances was—life preserving. But then I feared that the next unconscious step would be to stop writing about anything that had a political flavor to it, which meant after a while to stop writing altogether. So, having been invited to Columbia University as writer-in-residence for a semester, I made the decision to leave Argentina for good.

The American experience was very enriching. I taught at Columbia and New York University and managed to keep on writing about Argentina, since the distance gave me the necessary perspective. That went on until 1989 when *Black Novel with Argentines*, which took me over five laborious years to complete, was finally in the hands of the publishers.

In the first page of *Black Novel*, a murder is committed in the tradition of a thriller, but this soon becomes a thriller of the mind, or perhaps of the human soul. From the very beginning we know who the murderer is, and we know about the victim, but we have to work through the book in search of the motive of the crime. The man cannot explain—not even to himself—the reason why he did this, and in the process of writing, I myself had to delve deeper to get a glimpse of the truth. As usual, I had started the novel without an outline or preconception. The killer is an Argentine writer, living in New York on a grant. A serious enough guy, rather stiff and nonviolent, in spite of it all. The search for the motive takes place around the lower layers of life in Manhattan, and as the protagonists progress and regress in their search, glimpses of what had gone unsaid in Argentina, of the tortured and the clandestine detention camps and the disappeared, the corpses that could never be mentioned, started surfacing in the killer's mind. And in my mind as an author, I realized then how alienated, how distanced from our own selves we may become by not being able to acknowledge the terror going on around us, by not being able to express our fear and our fury.

This is why I keep on writing. Of course it seemed more glamorous when our lives were at stake, when we were threatened. Then we could feel like protagonists of sorts. And we could feel like we were doing something. There were the games we had to play. Somebody would make an appointment on the phone and give you the wrong hour and wrong place but we knew the code so we would meet earlier. Then you could only wait for that person for fifteen minutes and then you had to leave because something might have happened. All these phrases were exchanged that had nothing to do with reality, all these metaphors because you might be overheard. That gave us a sense of power. But the traps of oppression are always there. We have to be aware and look out for them even though we don't have this stimulation of fear or the adrenaline racing around us. But, too, that adrenaline might also lead us to silence, because at some point the fear can become uncontrollable. This is why I think what people in Argentina or Uruguay or Chile will tell you is true: that they didn't know what was going on; they didn't know all these people were being "disappeared," were being tortured and murdered. Not because they hadn't known in the beginning but because they had canceled it like some kind of Freudian negation. And that, again, is a trap the writer has to avoid. Either they can mollify you, put you to sleep with boredom with the political situation (but you don't have to allow yourself to be bored), or they can make you feel that with this terrible fear nothing can be said anymore.

I believe in writing with the body, but it is a gut feeling. It's difficult for me to conceptualize it. Of course, during that kind of writing or during the times of danger it was easier to know how and why we were writing with the body. When I wrote *Strange Things Happen Here* and was going to cafés and overhearing and writing in the presence of everybody, the body was at stake, the body was playing its part, and I knew what that meant.

I was then also discovering what political writing could be in its deeper sense, in its attempt to undo the slightest, smallest knot, the smallest innuendo that politicians were presenting you with. At that time I had in mind the advice that Rodolfo Walsh, that great and somewhat forgotten Argentine writer, had given me long before that. While I was still torn between Borges's line of non-commitment and the social realism advocated by the increasingly vociferous left, Rodolfo Walsh, who had been one of the persons to create *Prenza Latina* in Cuba, and who was a very committed political leftist, told me, "Forget the message. Forget whatever you have to say. Forget ideology. Forget everything but the story. If your ideology is strong enough, it will appear anyhow."

I also realized it was time for me to return to Argentina if I didn't want the marks that were already fading to dissolve forever, if I wanted to keep alive some kind of political gaze regarding my country. Baal Shem Tov's dictum, inscribed in Jerusalem at the entrance of the monument to the victims of the Holocaust, was ringing in my ears: "Forgetfulness leads to exile, while remembrance is the secret of redemption."

I don't regret the decision to return. There's always good political fodder available in these pastures; somewhat in excess, alas. At least for a writer who can be ironic. So among other texts, I wrote *Realidad nacional desde la cama* (*Bedside Manners*), national reality as experienced from the bed. But one can never withdraw, not even for a long-deserved rest. That's life in the letters of our times.

Rodolfo Walsh was one of the thirty thousand victims of the military dictatorship that ruled Argentina from 1976 to 1983. He died for his ideas but never contaminated his literature. He used his opinions in journalism and gave testimony in his books. He was killed while delivering an open letter to the newspapers denouncing the AAA. Rodolfo Walsh died for the letter. Few writers would allow his sacrifice to be in vain. I want to dedicate this paper to him.

Panel Discussion
Panelists: Robert Hegel, María Inés Lagos,
Liu Binyan, Margaret Sayers Peden, Anton Shammas

Anton Shammas: I would like to try to highlight some of the themes that Luisa Valenzuela talked about. I would put them under three rubrics: power, language, and memory. About this mutual infatuation between power and language, I would allude here to some of the ideas heard yesterday in the session with Mario Vargas Llosa about his relationship—or his language's relationship—to power. Underneath both language and power there is, of course, the memory of the writer. Luisa Valenzuela said that people want to forget in order to move on, but that they should stop and remember. So power tries to obliterate memory, and writers through language are trying to keep that memory alive.

Margaret Sayers Peden: Yesterday we discussed whether it is necessary to pose an opposition between committed writing and art. I wished personally, selfishly, I had had the opportunity to ask the writers involved what they considered their most subversive writing and what they considered their most artistically successful writing. I suspect it might be the same work. What impressed me, Luisa, in your remarks about avoiding Manichaeism was that it seemed to me that you were dissolving that opposition in everything you said: that language was the important thing. Then you quoted Walsh saying that you must write what you want to write and what comes out are your beliefs.

I'd like to make a detour. This is from the *Economist*, October 1991. Its title is "A Kiss on the Forehead." It begins, "In the popular imagination all Latin American fiction is magical realist and all Latin American writers are male. Not so." (I think we say, "Wrong.") "The first Latin American to be awarded the Nobel Prize for Literature was a woman, a Chilean poet, Gabriela Mistral. Now more and more Latin American women are claiming the right to wield not only the needle but the pen." (They use the needle a bit, too.) "The British Arts Council has just sponsored a tour dedicated to the work of two women, Claribel Alegría from El Salvador and Luisa Valenzuela from Argentina." (Do you find that amazing that there is a tour dedicated to these two women?) Their comments were: "Language has always been dominated by men. Adds Ms. Valenzuela, 'What we are trying to do is change its charge.' And in Ms. Valenzuela's novel *The Lizard's Tail*, the protagonist, Isabel Perón's megalomaniac Minister of Social Well-Being declares: 'Doubt is going to lead our country to ruin. Doubt has to be eradicated by decree. There is no room for doubt in history.' It is to challenge such authoritarian rigidity and the tyranny of certitude that these women write. I see writing as an act that will pull the rug from under the feet of the reader."

María Inés Lagos: I, too, am interested in what Petch [Peden] brought up. Which book or novel do you consider the most artistic and which the most political?

Luisa Valenzuela: I think I agree with Petch's theory. The book people like best is *Other Weapons* and it is very political. I think the best short story is "Symmetries." It is an attempt to address a subject as delicate as torture without making it blunt, without turning it into something pornographic. If one can succeed in this as Carolyn Forché has done in her poem "The Colonel," one has done something for the sake of literature.

Anton Shammas: In some of your works, you are dealing with this almost impossible task that writers burden language with, the language that has to convey to the reader this sense of pain. Elaine Scarry, author of *The Body in Pain*, has said that pain actually destroys language from within because there is no language to describe pain. Virginia Woolf once remarked that the English language has many words to describe love, affection, and other emotions, but falls short when it comes to describing a toothache. I would like you to address this topic of language, power, and memory, and also language, torture, and pain.

María Inés Lagos: I am interested in that, too. You finished your presentation with a dedication to Rodolfo Walsh. You also dedicated your novel *Bedside Manners* to him. This novel is a strong statement about the repression in Argentina after the military was overthrown. How was that novel received in Argentina? You said that people do not want to hear those stories. I must say I'm glad it's only ninety pages long because I don't know how one could continue reading such a painful account.

Luisa Valenzuela: It's so funny though, it's a farce.

María Inés Lagos: Yes, it is. But it's also very painful. I think that is the wonderful thing you do; all these things are present. That woman is under a politics in Argentina, but it is a politics that one can perceive from the bed. The situation is very funny. But how *was* it received in Argentina?

Luisa Valenzuela: There is one thing I want to tell you first. I dedicated the novel to Rodolfo Walsh, but I didn't say it. It says "To R. W. in Memoriam," because I didn't want to tint it politically. If I would have put the name Rodolfo Walsh there it would have been read in a special manner. The journalists don't want the novelists to be in possession of the political discourse.

Yes, it was taken as an amusing, political book, but it wasn't read deeply. I scare people in Argentina. I never say what they expect me to: as a woman, as a writer with some distance from them. I think that living abroad for a long time gave me another perspective. They feel this old thing, again, that was conveyed by the military: when you criticize a country, you criticize the countrymen. And it's not true—you criticize governments, certain attitudes. But everybody feels very uneasy when you're showing them a mirror, even if it's a distorted mirror, which is the one I use.

Liu Binyan: Luisa talked about the literary animal and the political animal. In its first thirty years of power, the Communist Party in China succeeded in making almost the whole nation of China into political animals, including writers. They were asked to serve politics, namely, to write works of propaganda. Anything concerning human nature, private life, or love, was prohibited. That made China much different, even compared to the Soviet Union and Eastern European countries. From the end of 1976 until now, writers have enjoyed a little more freedom. A unique phenomenon in China emerged: People eagerly and passionately began to place their hope in writers, waiting for them to write the truths of those thirty years. At the beginning of the 1980s, we writers and journalists did write some works to satisfy the people. But since the mid-1980s, more and more novelists have retreated from that mission under the influence partly from the West. As soon as China opened its doors, the writers, mostly the young writers, seized the literature of the United States as the representative literature of the outside world. Many fashionable theories and criticisms in the United States were used by those writers as an argument to defend themselves against the charge that they were distancing themselves from the society and the needs of the people. This is very sad. Also in the mid-1980s, the literature of Latin America was introduced into China, maybe because writers and poets of Latin America began to win the Nobel Prize. The young writers absorbed the form, for example, of magic realism, but without the substance or spirit. The retreat of the novelist, of fiction, from the life of the society made the literature of the past very popular in China. People wanted to know the truth, to get explanations for what happened and for what's happening in China.

Luisa mentioned the problem of memory. That is particularly important for the Chinese. You cannot imagine how the ordinary Chinese, the writers, and the scholars, were shut off from all the events that happened in China. Some things were taking place within the city where the writers were living and they didn't know about it. In the 1960s there was the famine. How many people died? More than *thirty million*! That's two Czechoslovakias! I believe that no more than a few *hundred* people in China knew that figure. Many people heard rumors that somewhere people died of the starvation created by Mao Zedong. But even those people who survived in the village where the other half of the population had died of starvation, even the surviving half did not know how many people died in the neighboring village. This is why, you see, even the leaders, the student leaders on Tian'anmen Square in 1989, didn't know the name of the dissident Wei Jingsheng. He was arrested at the beginning of 1979, sentenced to fifteen years in jail, where he remains. He has sacrificed so much for the Chinese people, but they don't know him. How sad this is.

The freedom enjoyed by the people of China is expanding, invisibly, imperceptibly, to include the freedom of the writers. Now the problem is not how much freedom you have, but how much you want to use that freedom. The Western influence of consumerism and commercialization is terrible. So many people in China are obsessed with making money, trying to make themselves millionaires. Some of them including writers can do that overnight. It doesn't seem that they are pained, or have some feeling of loss. No, they are satisfied. I believe there are writers trying to do something for society and at the same time trying to write valuable works. One of them recently wrote an article saying that the novel in China is going to die. So I deeply want all the lectures and discussions of this conference to be introduced into China to make our colleagues, Chinese writers and journalists, aware of the outside world and not just of the literature of the United States—and to know that the literature of the United States is not limited to just a few writers.

Robert Hegel: Not being a writer myself, I can only observe from the outside and comment on what I've seen, particularly in modern Chinese literature, because that's what I study most. Luisa Valenzuela said something that I think was most germane to understanding modern Chinese letters and the predicament in which modern Chinese writers find themselves, which has to do with writing under a politics. She said that when a war breaks out you have to choose sides. During the years that the Chinese Communist Party was growing, whether in Beijing or in some puppet government installed by the Japanese, it was clear that any opposition was justified. There were movements among writers to make a united front of different political perspectives and different levels of commitment to write against the enemy. The party, led by Mao Zedong, was quick to understand the importance of that and to press it forward. In 1942, at the infamous Yan'an Forum on Literature and Art, Mao Zedong made the opening and concluding statements, which swept under the carpet of history all other comments raised by the other writers present. What he said was that we have a task at hand and we have to devote all of our energies to defeating the enemy. The Japanese were defeated and a civil war ensued. The enemy became the Nationalist Party led by Chiang Kai-shek. The People's Republic was founded. And yet from that time until his death, Mao Zedong and his followers insisted that the war was still going on. The necessity to choose sides continued. One had to be engaged with the winning side, the power in Beijing, which produced a very curious manipulation of language.

During the Cultural Revolution, the last ten years of Mao Zedong's life, from 1966 through 1976, there was one writer, Hao Ran, whose work was officially endorsed by the leadership, published everywhere, and probably more widely read than any other living writer. Of course you got a readership when you were the only writer! He was, I suppose, at some point committed to the political program of the Chinese Communist Party. His writings became interesting to me as an outsider when I looked at how he used language. It became simpler and simpler and he used more and more slogans. There was less reality in his characters and more symbols. He was, at the end of his career in 1976, before Mao died, just manipulating symbols. I think he knew what he was doing. Then Mao died, the political situation changed, and there was an outpouring of writing called "scar literature" or "wound literature," whose characters, inevitably, were those who suffered under Mao's last years. Yet that movement passed very quickly, because that was the same kind of writing that Hao Ran had endorsed. It was writing with wooden characters, always with suffering victims, the evil Party people, and the evil leaders.

That was replaced by a more complicated literature, which did not have to express so directly the political sentiments of the writers. What it said to an outside reader was really very moving. It expressed the inner turmoil of how to deal with the guilt of having ignored exactly what Liu Binyan has been talking about—the fact that there were millions suffering, that they had been silenced and had not been allowed to read. There was a conference in 1983, in which one party leader got up and said, "You're free to write now. Write about anything." A certain number of people got up and said, "Thank you, we've been waiting for this." A couple of the older writers who had been most engaged in the 1920s when their lives were at stake for being active, like Ba Jin, for example, got up and said, "Okay, if we're free to write, let's see if we know how. We've had fifty years of writing with only one purpose, that is to be politically engaged. Do we know how to write in any way that could be considered art?"

There was a series of debates about why the Chinese hadn't won the Nobel Prize for Literature. Was it prejudice? Political factors? Pressure from the U.S.? I think it was because of the use of language and not just a matter of how well translated things are. Even those Chinese writers who try not to charge the language with a particular political sense write about political complexities that are hard for outsiders to understand. The writing will lose readers until Chinese writers become a part of international writing in general. And it's happening. There have been writers at the International Writers Workshop in Iowa from China for quite a few years now. In this way, language will take on an international bent. This has happened with film. *Red Sorghum* deals with the great myths, that, for example, the Japanese were horrible aggressors and the Chinese people stood up valiantly to resist them. The film exposed weaknesses in the Chinese character in a way that caused reflection on these sensitive issues. Because it gets you in the gut, it becomes much more universal and more capable of being understood by outsiders. Memory and language and engagement do go together. Good art in China is still likely to be political by virtue of what is embedded in the language rather than any chosen stance that's being depicted in the writing.

Anton Shammas: Luisa, how do you perceive this living under a politics of memory, so to speak. The politics that you lived under were, some would say, at a safe distance. But I would imagine from your point of view, you would interpret this distance in a totally different manner.

Luisa Valenzuela: I don't know how safe it is because what you are dealing with is your inner monsters in your writing, so you're not safe anywhere. I want to go back to that quote Petch read regarding the two literatures. I knew that was the way they were separating us from the mainstream, from the possibility of criticism. If they tell you, "Well, this is not Argentine literature," then whatever you say is invalidated. In that sense the distance will allow you to keep the memory because it won't be suffocated by whatever is going on at that time.

What Robert Hegel said, I thought, was very important, about this idea of a common enemy. They will find it for you. This is what frightens the United States probably. Communism is out, so where is the common enemy? When people began marching against the military (and this was a very courageous act in Argentina), the Falkland (Malvinas) Islands War was invented to deflect attention. Then there was a common enemy, England. Just imagine how good we would feel if we could fight England and win! I think that we have to be very wary when a common enemy appears.

Another important thing that Robert said was about the one main writer, how he became more and more wooden himself and could not use language anymore. It became slogans, commonplaces, clichés. But remember that the moment you utter one word, this word will betray you. That is what is marvelous about writing, allowing the betrayal to happen. This is why committed writing has to be very careful. If you don't allow the betrayal to happen, then you can be betrayed from the outside. We don't want this betrayal from the outside to happen in any way, so we *have* to allow the betrayal from the inside to happen, to see it, and to acknowledge it.

Anton Shammas: I suggest we go to the outside and listen to the audience's responses and comments.

Audience Member (Writer Ethan Bumas): My question is for Luisa Valenzuela. Would you discuss the importance of your friendship with two great Argentine writers: Julio Cortázar and Jorge Luis Borges?

Luisa Valenzuela: Cortázar was a very committed writer, but he also knew how to separate his political commitment from his writing. Separate and not separate—it is hard to explain. We spoke about everything except we didn't talk much about literature. Cortázar loved the Nicaraguan Revolution; I went to Nicaragua because of him.

With Borges you could only listen to Borges's monologues which were a great gift. You saw a great mind at work constantly, but no other mind could be at work at the same time. No other mind works at that level anyway.

Cortázar was much more humane. He was a real human being. I'm reminded of this piece I wrote for *La Nación* when Cortázar died. I had spoken with him shortly before. I asked him a very stupid question about literature, even though I had always avoided that subject with writers. He said that he had this novel in mind and that he wanted to take a sabbatical to write the novel. And I said, "Take the sabbatical." And he said, "No, but I have to go to Cuba, and then to Nicaragua, and then to Argentina. Then I'll take a sabbatical and write the novel." I asked another stupid question, "Do you know what the novel will be about?" (I knew he worked without a clear idea in mind.) He said, "No, I don't. But I often dream about it. I dream that the publisher hands me this book and I have it in my hands and it is the best book I have ever written. I leaf through it, understand it so clearly, and everything is there, all my thoughts, everything I ever wanted to say is there. And when I wake up, I realize it's a book not done with words but with geometrical figures." I thought that was absolutely fantastic.

Audience Member: It might please you to know that most Iranian writers have in the last several years been modeling themselves on South American writers, both in terms of form and content. I don't think your work has been translated into Persian, but many works, such as those by García Márquez or Fuentes, have reached the bestseller list. I was very surprised to see that there is nobody from the United States or Western Europe participating in this conference. It creates the assumption that where the political situation is more subtle, or where lip service is being paid to freedom of expression, writers can say whatever they want. A Swedish writer once told me: "I envy your situation because they censor you, they put you in prison, they torture you, they kill you. Here nobody gives a damn about what you say because the system works so subtly that you are entirely ignored." She said that there are two methods of censorship that the writer has to keep away from: official censorship and self-censorship. I think these subtle methods are worth exploring. In other words, is there a writer anywhere who does not live under a politics?

Luisa Valenzuela: Recently I heard Peter Matthiesen describe how his book about Leonard Peltier *In the Spirit of Crazy Horse* was censored in the United States. So we are always under a politics.

I have often heard what you describe: "You're lucky that you were persecuted and censored." I don't think censorship is any luck at all. The writer always has to find a way to say what goes unsaid, so censorship or not, we are always fighting something. On the other hand, you can be mollified by comfort; this is another war one has to fight.

But that nobody pays attention to you? To kill you is to pay attention to you? It's not because they've read you that they kill you, they kill you without even reading you.

María Inés Lagos: The International Writing Program at Iowa invited Nancy Morejón, the poet from Cuba, to participate in their workshops this semester. We invited her to come here to St. Louis. She was not granted a visa by the State Department. That is an example of how writers are censored here.

Margaret Sayers Peden: When Luisa said that a human being is a political being, I thought, what a remarkable statement, because I don't perceive the average North American citizen as being a political being. There are individual cases of censorship, there's no doubt about that. But, in my opinion, the worst censorship that the North American writer faces in a democracy is vulgarity, lack of taste, and lack of interest.

Audience Member (Marc Chénetier): I would like to speak to the subject of the last questioner. I was thinking of George Steiner's rather provocative idea that creativity flourishes under oppression because then it has to find channels that are not the usual ones. What I would like you to tell us, Luisa, is if you find, since you were submerged under the politics we are talking about, that this affected you in any way in the form you had recourse to? You mentioned that you had to speak in code, that you'd call someone and say, "I'll meet you there," but then you'd meet somewhere else two hours earlier. Did you find that this sort of circumvention generated a new form for your work? When you went back to the more regular situation, however disputable the transparencies of our democracies may be, did you follow formally a cycle that followed the political situation?

Luisa Valenzuela: I don't know. As a writer, I always look for what can't be said. I don't believe that much in the ineffable. Perhaps I played that game well because I was attracted to it. I try to force language and to play with connotations to the point of breaking the barrier of the unsaid, of the ineffable, to try to see what is beyond what is being said. I think you can find this in a work of mine like *El gato eficaz* (The efficient cat), in which I employed black humor and the grotesque. But you're always fighting that other thing, which is internal censorship. As a woman I know it perhaps much better than a male writer, because we had words we could not utter, bad words we couldn't say. We have to break all those barriers. Self-censorship came before the external repression.

María Inés Lagos: In 1990, you published (in Spanish) two novels: *Bedside Manners* and *Black Novel with Argentines*, both of which are highly political. One is more overtly political than the other, but *Black Novel* is also extremely political, if more subtle. In these narratives you're using two different ways of being under a politics. Would you tell us about the differences?

Luisa Valenzuela: Perhaps it does have to do with being inside and outside the country. The one that's more subtle politically I did not write in Argentina. *Black Novel with Argentines* was written from memory. For the other book, I had just returned to Argentina. I thought the country would be calm and would allow me to be reborn in my homecoming. Suddenly I was immersed in this national reality. It was the end of the regime of Raúl Alfonsín, and I thought that Carlos Menem might win the election, which I felt would be a disaster. But the transfer of power was not to happen until December and this was May, so I thought I would have some time to get used to being at home. Then there was an economic coup against Alfonsín, and the whole thing started crumbling very quickly: there was hyperinflation; they were raiding the supermarkets; the soldiers in the rebellious regiments had painted their faces; everything was happening at the same time. So that's why I wrote *Bedside Manners*. I really wanted to withdraw to bed and forget about it. But there is no way not to be under a politics, because it hits you everywhere, in the pocketbook even.

The book began as a play. I knew I wanted to describe what was happening to this woman on her bed, over her bed, to tell the story of the raids and the military exercises. But I wanted to work in depth, to say what goes unsaid, so then I transformed it into a novel. When I started working in depth I realized the importance of activity and passivity. I saw how active this woman was by being passive in her bed—acting in opposition to the military and fighting for social change. I wanted to show this opposition.

Anton Shammas: We'll take just two more questions. The first is from our friend Nuruddin Farah whom you'll meet in today's afternoon session. He's going to waste some of his ammunition now.

(Laughter)

Audience Member (Nuruddin Farah): I hope you had a very good laugh. I should say how much I enjoyed this presentation. Much of what you folks are doing in Argentina relates to what is happening in Africa and in a number of countries in the Middle East. I am reminded of how the writer, like a mole, hides secrets in a text. You've already done that by dedicating a book to R. W. and not to Walsh. There are a great many texts that are being read all over the world that have subtexts known only by the author, through initials, through undisclosed materials. Something I'm reminded of is a French friend of mine who is teaching in Algeria. She once announced to her Algerian colleagues, "Oh, Farah's novels will now finally be translated and you can all have them in French." The two Algerian professors took her aside and said, "We do not want Farah's books in French." She said, "But why?" They said that once they are in French or Arabic and they get into Algeria, then censors will read them, and they will become political books. Then the government will not allow the books to enter the country. As long as they are in English, a distant language, that will be fine. Even in places like Algeria or Egypt or Libya, language has been used more and more to hide texts, which are published in foreign languages. It creates that artificial literary distance. The moment that work is translated into a language of immediate importance then the story is different.

Luisa Valenzuela: It has to do with your readership. You can probably contaminate more minds in Algeria by being published in French than in English. Because the censors—although I don't think the censors read, actually—are being told this book is dangerous.

I want to pick up on the other subject of the secrets that one hides in the books. There are the internal personal jokes that one plants just to give codes to certain people. There are other secrets that one doesn't know are there but that one discovers rereading. Those secrets are very eerie because they might tell you things about yourself or about your writing that you don't want to know. Those are the ones that I think are the most interesting. That's what I fish for in my work. I get very scared at times, but I try to face that and let it happen. So again, I say, the inner censor is *the* censor you have to look for. That inner censor is there under the best of democracies. Fight that enemy, which is a very good one to focus on.

Audience Member (Writer Michael Castro): I heard an interesting dispute between Allen Ginsberg and Amiri Baraka a few years ago. Ginsberg was interpreting the notion of the writer and politics in terms of the CIA's harassment of him, and Baraka got upset and said, "I can write poems about what I see out of my window on the streets of New Jersey and can't get published because I'm told it's too political." You've talked a lot about how trying to say what goes unsaid is important to you. How do you understand the relationship between the transparency of evil that underlies any action or event, and the politics of having to find the phrases for what goes unsaid? Baraka seems to think that the transparency of evil is evident out there on the street. Is it about finding words for what everybody else doesn't look at, or is there a more subtle kind of repression?

Luisa Valenzuela: Baraka evidently has a very political mind that saw through whatever was going on in the street and said something that was threatening. Authorities feel very threatened by certain ways of seeing. So this is why—and it probably has to do with what Nuruddin was saying—certain writers see things that are uncomfortable for the powers that be. But it's there in one language or another. Somebody will always feel threatened. We writers are happy when that happens, because then we've hit our mark.

5   Savaging the Soul
of a Nation

Nuruddin Farah

■ Some of us debate whether or not to allow political matters to color our works of art, whether art can be in any sense political and still be art, whether to mix art and politics in our daily life, or whether to have anything whatsoever to do with politics. Some of us have the privilege, with our marketplace connections, our university and foundation patronage (with which I'm quite happy), our general irrelevance to the more malignant aspects of our governing institutions that encourage us to crawl into a comfortable corner and do our little angst acts for their entertainment or their therapy. The topic of today's session focuses on writers and writing not so privileged, and thus upon the problems and solutions of writers working under regimes that in fact criminalize the very act of expression.

About the time the folks in this hemisphere were winding up yet another of their internecine tribal wars—one of the bloodiest ever and provoked as usual in this uncivilized part of the world by savagery, ignorance, collective madness, primitive ideologies, greed, and racism—down in the southern hemisphere, Nuruddin Farah was born, son of an oral poet, in November 1945, in the land of Somalia, alas, all too well known to us today, even though it has taken a tragedy of unprecedented proportions to deflect our attention momentarily from our continuing fascination with the traditional and predictable European calamities. Nuruddin grew up multilingual, studied in a variety of schools, and was exposed to a kind of ideological pluralism. He was an Arab and a Muslim half of the day, a Christian the other half, and his days were such that there were always more than two halves in a whole. He studied in Somalia, Ethiopia, and India; taught in his homeland and in England, Italy, Uganda, and the

United States; and has traveled widely. He was a published novelist at the age of twenty-five and already in trouble. The book *From a Crooked Rib* focuses on the oppression of a young woman in a Somalia where women's rights did not exist and were not, dear sir, to be discussed. His trilogy of novels that followed, *Variations on the Theme of an African Dictatorship*, republished by Graywolf Press, displays Somali society under the recent dictatorship as corrupt and repressive. The consequent wrath of that government forced him into more or less permanent exile—an exile in which he is still, now condemned by crazed warlords. He has often described himself as a kind of nomad. The truth is that nomads are not rootless but merely have a different kind of rootedness, conservative in the closed patterns of their travels; but not so Nuruddin, whose travels, like those in his mind, are inquisitive, open-ended adventures, an exploration of all that the world has to show him. It's one such explorative adventure that has brought him here this week.

ROBERT COOVER, *Moderator*

Savaging the Soul of a Nation

In a telephone interview with the Italian newspaper *La Stampa* a few years ago, I had spoken of my feeling of foreboding, spoken of a civil war in embryo, of a Somalia whose people were very likely going to savage themselves into total extinction. Precisely a year later, I would forewarn the acting chairman of the Organization of African Unity, Uganda's President Yoweri Kaguta Museveni, that unless the outside world intervened, Somalia would be plunged into total anarchy. Siad Barre* had not been chased out of his citadel of disrepute by that time, and General Mohamed Farrah Aidid's men hadn't "taken" Mogadishu, nor had many of us heard of the names of the other warlords whose criminal activities have since held the nation's destiny to ignominious ransom. I remember suggesting to President Museveni, at the beginning of

*Editor's note: Mohammed Siad Barre died in exile in Lagos, Nigeria, on January 2, 1995.

January 1991, when I met him for several hours in the presence of his minister of state for external affairs, that he convene a meeting in Kampala under the OAU auspices and that he invite all the parties to the conflict. Left to me, I asserted, I would talk to anyone to avert a civil strife in Somalia; if need be, I would hold a dialogue with Satan, even if his human name is Siad Barre.

President Museveni spoke long-windedly, pontificating on the cynicism of his divided loyalties: because, as chairman of the OAU, he could not undertake any activity that might be construed as "interference in the internal affairs of another sovereign sister state." On the other hand, although his sympathies might be with the rebels whom he wished well, he had no choice but to reject my thesis that Siad Barre be invited not as a head of state but as another warlord. No doubt he was conscious of the ironies involved when he pointed out that until then none of the rebel movements in Somalia had submitted their accreditation to the OAU, the very body of which he happened to be chairman. He went on: "Pray, how can I justify putting them on par with a fellow head of state?"

Before we parted, President Museveni was kosher enough to advise me to heed the counsel of a politician who knew what he was talking about, adding, "Maybe you are a very good novelist, maybe an outstanding professor of literature, but when it comes to politics, you are too naive. If you want my advice, stay away from it."

I couldn't at first work out why my suggestion to think of Siad Barre as just another warlord had raised his hackles, but it wasn't long before I remembered that Museveni too had shot his way to power. At any rate, I hated the idea of parting with him on a note of discord or of falling out with him on matters of definition; and I desisted from asking him how anyone expected me to "stay away" from something as amorphous as politics. After several more attempts, we agreed on a modus operandi, namely that the Ugandan government's good offices would make contact with Siad Barre through the Somali Embassy in Kampala and would subsequently get in touch with the various factions via their representatives in Europe and East Africa with a view to convening an urgent OAU-sponsored meeting in Kampala.

However, when, after a fortnight, more than a thousand innocent civilians lost their lives in crossfire between the United Somali Congress and Siad Barre loyalists; when the Somali chargé d'affaires in Kampala chose to be discourteous, deciding not to honor Museveni's invitation; when it turned out that having dismissed my ominous remarks rather unceremoniously, he would not give a moment of his presidential time to the Somali crisis because he had his eyes glued, as did the rest of the world, to his television watching the fireworks, the bonfire, and fanfare of the Gulf War's laser-beam extravaganza; in short, when no action was taken on any of the points we had agreed on, I accused Museveni of ineptness. For his part, Museveni went on the attack at a press conference, describing me as a man with insatiable demands for controversies. Given that I am no equal to an African head of state in whose country I was living, I resigned my job as professor at Makerere University in Uganda and left for another country in the hope of revising a novel in the quiet of my seclusion, leaving politics to those who knew better than I.

I cannot help wondering what thoughts crossed Museveni's mind when not long ago he toured the unsightly devastation that has been visited upon Mogadishu; I cannot help asking myself if he remembers our conversation and how we might have been at the cutting edge in averting the crisis: if only he had paid heed to a naive writer's suggestion a few years ago.

In Somalia, anarchy is the order of the day, anarchy with its own rationale, and which perforce bows to its sense of power-mongering and to no one else's. The country is in irons, its fate tied to the destiny of its warlords, of whom there are as many as there are clans in the nation—warlords who are a law unto themselves, with no allegiance to traditional, scriptural, or secular power, only to themselves, to their ambition, that of imposing their will on a people refusing to afford them the acquiescence of the ruled. Do not these mad fools realize that you cannot govern a people against their volition, especially after a tyrant has been booted out? No doubt the mysterious workings of a warlord's mind are not for me to unravel, except perhaps in a roundabout way, and because I am unable to negotiate my way round the blind bends of a tyranny of total helplessness, I might as well explain why I prefer the version of the Cain-killed-Abel myth in which the two brothers fight over the inheritance rights of a property that neither is destined to inherit. Granted, a couple of significant lessons to be culled from the Cain-killed-Abel myth is that human beings are the only species known to be "mass murderers" and that death has a name in Somalia, a name to which it answers: that of a warlord who's caught the virus of insanity.

Do warlords have an organized form of politics in the shadow of whose nebulae a writer might pursue his vocation? Would it be wise for a novelist who's lived in exile for eighteen years to fly straight into a city replete with bandits who've been infected with the epidemics of lunacy, with marauders who operate on a free-for-all basis without regard to human dignity or life and who engage in an insane rivalry of fratricidal overkill?

I've read somewhere that the first shot of World War I was fired somewhere in Bosnia. If that is so, then perhaps we are in a position to isolate the one event out of which all this anarchy arose, a shot which was fired at a checkpoint outside Mogadishu's city limits by one or other of the militia movements. And if, as they say, the devil hides in the detail, then let's smoke him out by stating right away that the shot was fired on the afternoon of the very morning Siad Barre fled the citadel of his corrupt power base. No one is certain who gave the order, or if any of the warlords meant to exploit the all-pervasive tension. I'm more than certain we would tell a different tale about Somalia today if the shot hadn't been fired.

Sadly, I hear the echo of the first shot and replay it very often in the ears of my recall. And I remember being overwhelmed with the oddest of sensations, as if an insect began to crawl down my spine, towards the nether regions of my self-reprimand. When someone first told it to me, I remember a most awkward sensation, as if the arch-angel of death had served his notice on me; as if I died a quick death, but just before doing so, was able to think ahead: and I saw corpses, hundreds, thousands of unburied bodies, and a million people fleeing a savaging crisis. I spoke of these worries to a Ugandan friend, who put it to me that I had better not speak of any of that to anybody. My Ugandan friend talked of my pent-up anxieties, that of a national who is preoccupied about the survival of his country. But why did the firing of that first bullet shock me so?

Bullets and guns, disruptive instruments of coercion, have been imported by one ruling oligarchy or another for a purpose, that of pacifying people into submission. I associate so much destruction with that single bullet, which keeps ringing in the ears of my memory, and I think of a world brought to its knees; and in the echo of its distant sound I hear the pleas of the dying, I hear the whimpers of dying babies, whimpers not so very different from that of a slaughtered goat. And when I replay the ringing horror, I hear in the imagination of my recall that first shot which was fired by the colonial powers to pacify the country so as to exploit it. After all, a hawk needs powerful claws to catch its prey, doesn't it?

A Somali proverb has it that a coward gathers far too many sticks. Tyrants, whether they appear in the guise of colonialists or post-colonialists, have a way of displaying their cowardice by amassing machines of destruction—in fact, the more insecure the state, the more weapons it accumulates. It follows then that the first to bring large quantities of weapons into Somalia were the European powers; the next to do so was Siad Barre. In an interview I gave to a London-based African magazine, I remember cracking what I then took to be a joke: that every weapon imported into our continent must carry a warning: that bullets maim; that guns kill; that tanks make coups d'état possible. Why, cigarettes bear a warning alerting smokers and nonsmokers alike of the dangers they might cause. Now, guns aren't locally made any more than the toxic waste that has recently been exported to Somalia by Europeans exploiting the suicidal nature, the disruption of civic society. Because one of the marauding warlords has more guns at his disposal, the other—to finance the maverick ambition of equaling his firepower—sells a few kilometers of the coast under his domain. Between brothers, says a Spanish proverb, two witnesses and a notary. What a tragedy!

In an article I published in Britain's *Guardian* in November 1989, I expressed the opinion that come December 1990, Siad Barre would be overthrown, and that I would be driving my newly acquired vehicle overland all the way to Mogadishu. That was not to be. Perhaps it doesn't matter now, but Siad Barre was chased out in January 1991, a month later than I had predicted. However, although I had not foreseen how much wanton violence the tyrant's departure would unleash, I had started working on a novel about civil wars at a period when I didn't believe my own prognostics. Somehow I sensed that once Somalia collapsed into absolute anarchy, my novel would die in tandem with my dream, that of returning home.

There is a pattern to civil wars. People and the truths that they hold closest to their hearts become casualties, and both suffer the cruelty of distortion. Novels have their intrinsic truths, poetic notions not given to the impetuosity of impulse or one's surrender to the epidemic lunacy all around. Somalia: a country turned into a madhouse. Is this why I've had to put the novel about the Somali civil war on hold, until sanity returns, until reason reigns absolute?

Over the years I've written my novels about a country bearing resemblances to Somalia. As a novelist I've dwelled in the country of my imagination. It hasn't mattered to me for two decades whether or not I knew the physical layout of the cities that served as the background of the stories I told; for years I've been able to conjure up images of Mogadishu, a city with whose residents I've managed to get in touch at will. Admittedly, there have always been gaps in my anthropological knowledge of these people's day-to-day existence, but this didn't deter me from imagining them and working them into a text as characters. Of late, however, I've failed in raising in them an instinct of humanity: maybe because of the psychic epidemics, and maybe because what's been happening in Somalia defies my understanding. And I think of death, my death, as the first bullet rings again and again in the ears of my recall. I wonder if it is me who's died and not my novel!

Panel Discussion
Panelists: Robert Coover, Ron Himes, Liu Binyan, Anton Shammas, Richard Watson

Robert Coover: Nuruddin spoke of how his current work seems to have been swallowed up by the realities of his country, that even as he imagined a quite violent work—one dealing with civil strife—the violence of the country itself overswept this project in a way that is not the same thing as history catching up to our ideas, but rather our imagination being swamped by the unimaginable activity of the world at large. Nuruddin, in spite of being in exile for nearly half his life, has continued to write about the country from which he has been exiled. He described how his imagination was still able to remake or rebuild the locations that perhaps have changed beyond his own recognition of them. What is the impact upon the imagination of a writer who has to write under a politics? To what extent can he search for freedom and how does he come to focus upon something within this experience in which he can begin to do his own writing? Let me turn to a writer who has faced somewhat similar circumstances and ask him to respond to Nuruddin's remarks and also to reveal to us in what similar ways he might himself have worked out these problems. Anton?

Anton Shammas: I would like to highlight some of the points that Nuruddin alluded to in his presentation, but more so in his fiction and sometimes in his nonfiction writings. I am very interested in talking about Somalia with a Somali writer who was apparently the first to write a book in a newly invented Somali alphabet, in the early 1960s was it, Nuruddin?

Nuruddin Farah: Early 1970s.

Anton Shammas: This brings the sensation of using a newly invented script in order to write down an oral tradition. In some of his writing Nuruddin uses this theme of orality and literacy, and the way the literacy is used by literate societies in order to impose their rule over oral societies. Somalia is a perfect example of the vicious invention of the alphabet; modern powers and governments are using that invention in order to perpetuate states of mind that are abhorrent to any human being. Nuruddin has mentioned that, for instance, two Bosnian children would get more attention in the American media, or anywhere else for that matter, than the whole nation of Somali people starving to death. The *New York Times* reported that it wasn't until more than a year into the Somali tragedy that network news bothered to pay any attention to that end of the world. This piece, written by Walter Goodman, a critic for the *New York Times*, says that it is "very difficult to imagine a million or more white children dying in some part of the world without attracting troops or American reporters and more television pictures no matter how difficult or dangerous the job."

Nuruddin talked about his meeting with President Museveni. This brought to my mind a famous story from *A Thousand and One*

Nights, and by way of commenting on Nuruddin's situation, I would just like to remind you of that story, because I think this is the best way to answer the question of what a writer should do under a politics. I hope that you are in a good mood to listen to tales at this siesta time—don't go to sleep. It's a story about King Yunan and his sage Duban. King Yunan had a severe case of leprosy and his doctors and physicians couldn't do anything about it; medicines did not help, and ointments did not work. To make a very long story short, though this is not in any way how the storyteller in *A Thousand and One Nights* would put it, the sage Duban invents this miraculous mallet. (It's a game of ball and mallets that kings used to play, especially throughout the pages of *A Thousand and One Nights.*) The sage put the medicine in the handle of that mallet and ordered the king to play the game all day, only then would he recover. And, as is always the case in stories, that is exactly what happens. Now this miraculous event arouses the suspicion of the king and especially one of his envious wazirs who conspires to turn the king against the sage Duban. Fearing that Duban would some day take over, King Yunan orders his execution. I will just read you the final section of that story because I think it speaks to Nuruddin's coming from an oral culture and then taking upon himself the limitations of the alphabet, living under or away from, but still fearful of a regime. In *Maps,* one of his novels, he talks about the brutal force of the written tradition imposed on an unwritten tradition. He gives examples: the Amharic-speaking people, for instance, had a written tradition and could spread their power over peoples from the oral tradition such as the Somalis. And as I said, this is my reflection on our topic today.

"The sage Duban entered, carrying an old book and a kohl." (A kohl is a cosmetic used by women to darken their eyelids.) "So he carried an old book and a kohl jar containing powder. He sat down, ordered a platter, poured out the powder and smoothed it on the platter. Then he said to the king, 'Take this book, your Majesty, and don't open it until after my execution. When my head is cut off, let it be placed on the platter and order that it be pressed on the powder. Then open the book and begin to ask my head a question, for it will then answer you. There is no power and no strength save in God, the Almighty, the Magnificent. For God's sake, spare me, and God will spare you; destroy me, and God will destroy you.' The king replied,

'I must kill you, especially to see how your head will speak to me.'
Then the king took the book and ordered the executioner to strike
off the sage's head. The executioner drew his sword and, with one
stroke, dropped the head in the middle of the platter, and when he
pressed the head on the powder, the bleeding stopped. Then the sage
Duban opened his eyes and said, 'Now, your Majesty, open the book.'
When the king opened the book, he found the pages stuck. So he
put his finger in his mouth, wetted it with his saliva and opened the
first page. He kept opening the pages with difficulty until he turned
seven leaves. But when he looked in the book, he found nothing
written inside, and he exclaimed, 'Sage, I see nothing written in this
book.' The sage replied, 'Open more pages.' The king opened some
more pages but still found nothing, and while he was doing this, the
drug spread through his body—for the book had been poisoned—
and he began to heave, sway, and twitch."

I will talk about this more later.

Robert Coover: Were you able to follow the tale? I'll ask Liu Binyan
to comment.

Liu Binyan: I can fully understand what Nuruddin said here, and I
share his feeling. What is happening in Somalia mirrors the recent
history of China. The first half of the twentieth century was full of
all kinds of wars. I personally have lived through twenty-three years
of war: nine years of civil war and fourteen years of the war against
the Japanese invasion. It is not just history but reality. It seems to
me that the futures of both Somalia and China will depend on not
only how powerful people will take part in the resistance and struggle
against the evil but also on whether the people will be wise enough
to deal with each other properly. What we Chinese dissidents are worried about is not how long the present regime, the Chinese Communist Party, will be in power. The question is what will happen in
China after that regime falls.

The biggest destruction made by the Communist Party regime is
of human beings and the morality and spiritual quality of the people.
I want just to mention one fact which I think will reflect this. We
have never had a phenomenon such as today when millions of people
are trying to get out of China, and not because they are poor. Many

of them are rich. They spend over $30,000 to buy fake visas to get out of China. I am told that in New York City, an average of 6,000 to 8,000 illegal Chinese refugees arrive each month. Every day more than 200 illegal refugees come to New York! Why are people choosing to get out of China? Because forty years of rule by the Chinese Communist Party made the country disgusting to them. People tend to relate their resentment toward the regime to the society, to the people. That's why right now there is so much destruction against the people in China; it is rarely reported in the mass media. Only now are they trying to find some means to cure the spiritual crisis of the people. Cynicism prevails everywhere in China. The words "ideal," "responsibility," and "commitment" have become the targets of irony. A writer from Hunan province, a talented and committed one, recently wrote an article, "The Death of the Novel in China," in which he tells how the Chinese novel lost its soul at the same time that Chinese writers lost their souls. It's painful to say and to hear but it is reality.

Robert Coover: A student of mine just came back from China. She was born there and left only some years ago. She went back to look up her old childhood haunts, which were the camps to which many had been sent during the Cultural Revolution. She also went to see writers and poets and to find out what was happening in the arts. There are a couple of underground magazines getting started again, but the main problem is how to make money with these things. What she found was the cynicism and the avarice that Liu Binyan is speaking of, this idea that writers with grander motivations are to be ridiculed. Okay, off to theatre. Ron?

Ron Himes: Nuruddin raised some questions for me, particularly about literacy versus orality. The task we have in the theatre is the presentation of something that is literate but in an oral tradition. How do we present these literate thoughts to people who need an oral presentation? In listening to him talk about the warlords in Somalia, it made me think about the warlords in African America. How do we speak to the warlords and to people who have come from an oral tradition and have had a literate tradition placed upon them? How in their illiteracy do we speak to them? Are we able to communicate any types of messages to them so that we are able to move forward?

Robert Coover: Some remarks from Richard Watson.

Richard Watson: I'm going to speak as an American writer. Bob Coover, with his incredible *Cat in the Hat for President* and *A Public Burning*, is the one who should speak as someone who has written novels committed to political concerns. American writers usually are very apologetic in this company, for reasons that you all know. When I thought about writers and writing under a politics, it seemed to me that in America that means that we are beneath consideration if not contempt. What has happened for a lot of minor writers like myself, is that we have written about inner things, we have gone underground. The first novel of mine that was published, *Under Plowman's Floor*, is about going underground in Kentucky where a man explores a great cave. His contact with the larger world of politics is nil. He gets his community from a small voluntary group. I pursued that theme in a second novel that was published in the 1970s, *The Runner*, in which a man becomes obsessed with jogging, runs around in a circle, and then he goes into himself. He moves into the interior, under a politics that doesn't care. I think this attitude characterizes a great deal of American writing in the last twenty to thirty years.

There's another kind of writing that I've been involved with besides fiction: committed writing in the environmental movement in the United States. I want to make some contrasts with what Nuruddin has said and to come to a kind of analogical conclusion that I find very pessimistic. In the late 1950s a number of us began working for the Wilderness Act in this country, which we did manage to get passed. The problem is that although that law is on the books, it is very seldom enforced. We are faced with the opening of parks and national forests to strip mining. I wrote a great deal for the Nuclear Regulatory Commission, which had me on a panel with a group of people who were looking into America's goals for high-level radioactive waste disposal. That was in 1975. One of the first things we found was that there are hundreds of reports that duplicated what we were finding. They knew what to do in 1945 with nuclear waste: bury it deep, somewhere, almost anywhere. The larger the constituency that knows about these things, the more likely it is that something could happen. I don't believe that all that writing, those tons of reports, will have any effect because it will cost billions of dollars more than the profits of the nuclear power plants to put them in disposal units. Now wherever there is a nuclear power plant, there is a de facto radioactive waste site: put a fence around it and tell people to stay away. That's what it will come to. A tremendous amount of writing and political activity has gone on in this country to save environmental resources and treasures. Then one day the other side wins. The people cutting the trees down must win only once. When the forest is clear-cut, say, or a piece of the Amazon rain forest is taken out, the ground then turns into hard, dry, red clay and there is no reclamation of this. The battle is about resources that cannot grow again.

Now this brings me to what Nuruddin said. We have seen all over the world, and now in Somalia, dictatorships arise, with thousands, millions of people killed. He says most depressingly, that he believes that the African character wants dictatorship. What you see now in Bosnia, in Serbia, and what was Yugoslavia, is the continuous escalation of what human beings can do to other human beings and get away with. Once the centralized control was taken out of Eastern Europe, an enormous number of ethnic battles started, although for seventy years a lot of them had been held down. The pessimistic conclusion that I want to draw here, parallel to what Nuruddin is saying is: What's left when you lose? What's going to be in Somalia after these present warlords are taken out? Will something else grow there, or has the land been made into desert in Bosnia or Serbia or Northern Ireland? Can you start anew? Are there new seeds there? What has happened is that there is ground on which these horrors have already occurred and you can't start afresh. Nuruddin can't go home.

Robert Coover: I've heard a lot of despairing remarks. Richard was careful about distinguishing between the two sorts of writing that he does as if one is more or less irrelevant to the major issues at hand. We heard from Liu Binyan about the lack of purpose in narrative art in the midst of these situations under a politics. Anton questions the very power of language itself and the tyranny of literacy. What might be solved if you had to do it by way of some sort of deep ionizing medium? I was thinking about Nuruddin's travels, how he described why he made them. I think one reason he did it was to look for a place that was orderly enough to impose upon himself a discipline and get the books done, but in doing so, feeling at times as though he were abandoning something that was important to accomplish. And in the end, abandoning the very appeal that anarchy has on the imagination.

Nuruddin Farah: Uh, before—

Robert Coover: Excuse me, Nuruddin, please go ahead.

Nuruddin Farah: I'm actually quite surprised at the inadequate responses that I'm getting from the panelists, each of whom seems to be looking at his own navel and not bothering about the questions, the basic questions, which we must be asking ourselves. A country has collapsed into total anarchy, it is going to go out of existence. Anton Shammas, who is a good friend of mine, speaks about some king who is poisoned through oral literacy. Ron speaks of what to do with oral literature. We're not talking about that. We're speaking about the responsibility of the individual as an individual, the responsibility of the writer as a writer, to a crisis such as Somalia which happens to be the first of its kind anywhere in the world—a state which existed and collapsed into absolute total anarchy. The environment is fine, but the environment can only be fine if the relationship is worked out in such a way that it is linked to the toxic waste that's being dumped in Somalia. What we're actually saying is that what's happening in Somalia is the responsibility of the people who created it, and the people who created it are *you* sitting here—outsiders, who first brought the guns and the ammunition and the hate, and who continue to do that, thinking only about themselves and about their tomatoes and their drinks and so on and so forth. So this is the question that I'm speaking about. It's not an intellectual thing for me.

Robert Coover: Yes, but—not to take up the cudgels on behalf of my fellow panelists who I'm sure can handle this on their own—it's a little bit like the situation in which television destroys the human imagination so that eventually everybody takes on a kind of martyr complex vis-à-vis the world and its tragedies. How is my responsibility to be connected to these acts? When you point the finger at us and say that we are the ones responsible for the situation in Somalia you are ignoring your own effort to speak, because you had the power to do so with a person who had an opportunity to do something. The panelists were trying to find a way to deal with a topic, that is, writers under a politics, that they themselves have not suffered. They have not lived the Somali experience. I think they came prepared with a few thoughts to say upon the general topic. Perhaps we should follow Nuruddin's lead and respond directly to his concerns about the circumstances he outlines in his paper. Did I see a hand up?

Audience Member (Leon Foote): Not to diminish what Mr. Farah was saying, I think that when Richard Watson refers to an American writer not being taken seriously, I wonder if he's confining that to the European-American writer, because somebody like Amiri Baraka, for example, cannot be published. That to me is a political statement by the publishers that what he has to say is too political. I think we're trying to explain away the validity and the political nature of what writers do here today.

Robert Coover: Richard?

Richard Watson: No, he's perfectly right. I should have said the United States. Latin American and South American writers are much more engaged than the writers I was talking about.

Robert Coover: He also brought up that we writers in this country suffer from a sort of tyrannical operation, namely that of a market-place, and its reluctance to get itself involved with issues that are either too controversial or not profitable enough to exploit, using Amiri Baraka as an example of someone who is having trouble getting published. How do you feel about it, Nuruddin, when, in an audience such as this, in the middle of middle America, there is an effort to say that we are all in the same boat. Do you feel that that's taking upon ourselves something we have no right to?

Nuruddin Farah: No, I think we're all in the same boat, and—if I've lost my temper, I'm sorry—the reason I thought I should say this is because I have spoken about not the death of an author in the way critics have been trying to kill authors off so that they could teach whatever they wanted, I was speaking about the death of an author because the country which the particular author has been writing about has been rendered nonexistent. Bill Gass asks me to sign a piece of paper in defense of Salman Rushdie who is living in order for us to keep him from dying. A *country* has died. Are you willing to put your signature to help the survival of a country? In other words are we always thinking only about the profession which we pursue, the friends whom we have, or do we think of a larger world of which we are part? I've shown you how the environment in Somalia is linked directly with the environment in the U.S.

Robert Coover: Yes, but to whom are we directing this? How do we speak to the warlords? We know who we are speaking to in Salman Rushdie's case. We are speaking directly or indirectly to the Ayatollah, the ex-Ayatollah, and the present regime in Iran. There is a very specific sense of where this oppression is coming from and how we might speak to that person.

Nuruddin Farah: If enough attempt is made to speak to the warlords in Somalia here or anywhere else in the world, as much of an attempt as in Yugoslavia, then we will get somewhere. The reason why we're not getting anywhere is we're always thinking about ourselves as writers, who want to survive next week and write another book and get a good review perhaps, but not about the death of a country.

Robert Coover: Anton has asked me for the table here.

Anton Shammas: I have two different answers but I'm not sure to what extent they are going to be helpful to the discussion so I will try to be very mild. I'm shocked at your reaction to this. Your reaction assumes that not only the panelists but the people who are sitting there have no sympathy at all to the cause that you are bringing to our attention. It is not only a problem of this audience here but a problem of information and who uses the media and what people do with the information they have. Now I'm also shocked in listening to you today, because I was hoping that my first reading of your beautifully written piece would be wrong. The minute you reacted like that, I thought, "Oh my God, I was right." Nuruddin, I think you are—at least in this piece, I haven't met with you for a few years, I don't know what's happened in the meanwhile—infatuated by power the way Mario Vargas Llosa is. I think at your meeting with the prime minister of Uganda, you wished at that moment that you were not a writer but somebody else. Now I tried to allude to that. I am also shocked that somebody like you, a master storyteller, does not read between the lines of things that should not be stated openly. That was what I was trying to tell you in this story about the killing of the king by using the blank book. I thought there was a message there. You can't do anything about that unless you do what this sage did but in a different way. But we don't talk about these things openly. We think about them. The main thing I'm trying to say is that I hope I'm wrong but I think you've been lured by power. I'm afraid for you and I'm afraid for your writing and I hope I'm wrong in that.

Audience Member (Breyten Breytenbach): I'm afraid I have to agree with Anton to some extent. One must be very careful. Somebody once said that there are two forms of corruption: corruption of power and corruption of suffering. For us, coming from certain parts of the world, we run the risk of losing our souls in this turmoil of suffering. It's true what you say. I think Boutros-Ghali pointed it out in his own way: There is a rich man's war going on in the ex-Yugoslavia and there's a poor people's war in Somalia that other people don't care about. That's true. But I think we must, especially for that reason, think very carefully about the causes and consequences and what we can possibly do. For a start I wouldn't agree with you that this is the first time a country has erupted into anarchy. For example Liberia already has. We have to ask ourselves why this is allowed to happen. Why isn't someone doing the utmost to stop it from happening? You yourself pointed out in your paper: We have a personal role in this tragedy, as Africans. What are Somalis doing? It's not the fault of the people here. That's a rhetorical trick. Yes, they can help, of course, yes, they must do so, and many of them will. But it's up to us. It's not because they are strong that we are weak, it's because we are weak that they are strong. I think it was a cheap shot to take at the fellow panelists. Listen to them. They are not simply applying their own labels, not any more so than you are or than I am. Each in his own way showed a tremendous amount of empathy towards what you were saying and I think you should be grateful for that. It's something very precious.

Richard Watson: Nations have collapsed from the beginning of history. Take the seventeenth century, take the Roman Empire—this is not a unique event.

I want to clarify the analogy I made which I thought was very straightforward. In some of the political battles in this country, people fight for a forest, for example, but once it's cut down, the battle is over. Once Somalia collapses, the battle is over. Now something will rise out of it perhaps, but what? One can't go back to the way it was. What those people have to do is raise something new. That is the point I wanted to make.

Audience Member (Marc Chénetier): I'd like to try and cool things down a little bit, because I think that since this is a writers' conference, it might be interesting to focus on words. The gentleman who asked the first question referred to the case of Amiri Baraka. Apart from the respect I have for him as a writer, the political ideas he has been promulgating over the last ten to fifteen years are very similar to the sort of ideas that kept our friend Liu Binyan under the lid for twenty years.

I wasn't surprised by your reaction, Nuruddin. I think it is excessive, but that's okay. I think it was beside the point that brings us together, but I'm not saying that it was unimportant *at all*. It was Confucius who said that the first task is to give back to words their real meaning before anything else.

Anton mentioned "the tyranny of literacy." I object to this notion unless one changes it into the tyranny of the printed word. Literacy is a liberating thing and no one is going to tell me that it is tyranny. It is the only tool we have. It might be good if we change the vocabulary.

The second word I heard used a little bit outside of the normal usage is guilt. I take my politics raw, and it is not the place here for me to say what I do in the political realm, but I do resent being lumped as a guilty culprit in this abominable scene. I have reasons to believe that I'm not exactly liable to bear that accusation. But this would be another debate.

The third misuse of a word is the notion of personal responsibility. What I was fascinated by in your talk, Nuruddin, was this: at least twice you were compelled to say that you had as a writer to step aside from your usual labor in order to do something more pressing. You mentioned your abandoned manuscript, that you spoke with this person of responsibility. What I am interested in hearing from you is how you see the writer's responsibility as a writer in this situation? When Richard said the seeds are all gone and perhaps nothing will grow—are you not the soul? Are you not the one who keeps the memory of the people and who tells stories anew so that people will have stories to tell, even though it looks like your country is being eradicated from the face of the earth? Isn't that the writer's responsibility? I do understand what Anton meant when he said that perhaps your extremely urgent mood to meet that person of power was doomed to fail. Maybe it was not what you are meant to do. Would you please react to this?

Nuruddin Farah: I laid the responsibility at your door with the understanding that we share the writer's concern. I've also spoken not of writer's block, and not of the death of a novel, but the death, or the killing, of the imagined country by somebody else. I have come appealing to you to respond to the death of that author and to somehow help with this particular person continuing to exist—at least in the imagination. Perhaps I went on the attack with regard to Anton, but he speaks of something completely different from my idea of literacy. Ron speaks of imposing a literary heritage on a people. Now the Somalis were a very literate people—as a matter of fact in terms of oral literature, they are great oralists. What I'm speaking about is how responsible we are towards another writer who comes and says to you, "An author is dead." What are you going to do about it? Not an author dead in the way that authors are generally dead, physically, or not an author dead because critics have decided to kill him or her, but because he is being deprived of his source of imagination. That is where the responsibility lies. The country as imagined continues to exist in the books. If you want to reconstruct the city of Mogadishu today, the only way you can do that is to read my second novel, which gives you the names of all the streets. Now all this has been destroyed. How can you as a community of writers help me in this regard? This is the question I was asking.

Robert Coover: Anton's little parable from *A Thousand and One Nights* seems to resonate, partly because of the blankness of the pages the king is turning, with a force that is ambivalent and doesn't supply an answer as much as a kind of hope that the writer's task and role are not changed if the whole world is erased behind him. If all his friends and sources of his imagination are taken away from him and he is disempowered in all ways, I don't think it changes his approach to the world. That's how we approach the world. We don't get ourselves elected to office. We sit down with paper or computers or video cameras to accomplish some sort of art object that responds to that world. My guess is that that book will yet be written. Do I have more questions from the audience?

Audience Member (Reporter Rebekah Presson): I would like to know if you perceive a change in what you have written. In your novels there is a pervasive theme of the emasculation of the Somali people, primarily by outside forces. It's clear that you as an author lay blame for the acceptance of that fate upon people who continuously tell themselves that they have no choice but to go along with the corruption and evil in the system, because they have to take care of their families and feed their hungry children. There is also the theme of how the Muslim religion helps reinforce the emasculation and the acceptance of the horrors placed upon the people. These books were written before things became the way they are now. Have your opinions on what happened in Somalia, or who is responsible for what happened in Somalia, altered? It seems to me you place the blame on the Somali people in your books.

Nuruddin Farah: My opinion has not altered. I said it today, that the first responsibility lies with the people themselves. It's they who place the curse upon themselves. We're talking a great deal about a writer's commitment, not only to art but also to politics and to the life being lived around himself or herself. I was talking about the human commitment to the continuation of the Somali humanity, if you want to call it that. Perhaps I've been clumsy in understanding the subtleties of *A Thousand and One Nights* today and the wisdom—

Anton Shammas: Let it go. Forget about *A Thousand and One Nights*.

Nuruddin Farah: —or the wisdom being hurled in my direction by—because now I am definitely angry at myself or others, and I think that novel is coming back and—

Robert Coover: I said so.

(Applause)

Nuruddin Farah: —it will get written before the end of the year. Let it be known to Breytenbach that without the continuous encouragement and support from other people, whether they come in the shape of readers or they come in the shape of givers of allegories in order to elucidate points of departure or return, writers have often depended upon the larger community and not on writers who always think only about themselves. If I spoke to another group of persons and not writers, they would probably have spoken differently about this particular issue.

Audience Member (Lorin Cuoco): Nuruddin, this audience is not just made up of writers.

Robert Coover: We are finding ways of tying up themes here: Bill Gass remarked that sometimes the best source of creative energy is rage.

Audience Member (Breyten Breytenbach): In your essay, you talk about the disappearance of a country, the death of an author. We can see you are in anguish. I think you are clumsy, perhaps, in the way you share it with us. But don't misunderstand us. We could hear you very clearly. I would agree this is something writers ought to be very concerned about. You mentioned the case of Salman Rushdie, and about the petitions to have him protected, to try to raise money to make it possible. Shouldn't we as writers in some way or other think more collectively, more coherently about what we can do to help our fellow writers who find themselves in the situation you find yourself in? Many others have been there. Perhaps it's about time we gained a much broader base and started thinking about what we can do.

Nuruddin Farah: If I came to you and said I had no money, I'm quite sure that some of you would put your hands in your pockets, if you see what I mean. This is a question much, much larger than myself.

Ron Himes: When I was much younger my grandfather told me to be careful about preaching to the choir. I am neither a writer nor do I consider myself in any way a scholar. My comments were those of an artist of the theatre—but more of a lay person. Had this room been full of writers, I think that what would have been happening was a wonderful sermon to the choir. What my comments were attempting to address was that there are a number of times that we try to transmit ideas, through theatre or literature. Who do we actually wind up speaking to? We have to be careful of finding a way to communicate. When we transmit our ideas, we have to make sure that those ideas can be picked up by the people who can take them and do something with them.

Audience Member: I was pleased to see this passionate outburst because until that moment I didn't really understand what it was like to be under a politics, to suffer like that. I think we shouldn't be afraid to have fingers pointed at us. I need some of that passion to be able to understand how I can be a better person. I don't think anyone should be afraid of that.

Audience Member: I have been thinking about what writing does under various circumstances and how it enlightens people. I was thinking of the many purposes of art. One is to serve as a memorial. It makes me think of a photographer, I believe his name was Roman Vishniac, who went to Poland in the late 1930s before Hitler moved in. He smuggled in a camera and photographed people. The photographs became a memorial to those people—I believe the book is called *The Vanished World*. That is something that art, that writing can do. I think what we're talking about now is preventing that situation, but perhaps this is not the forum.

Robert Coover: Do you mean that literature is not the forum—

Audience Member (continued): We need something more immediate that reaches a lot of people. If there is the expectation that something is actually to be done—

Robert Coover: —that the novel is not apt to serve this purpose?

Audience Member (continued): If I want to feed my family, I go into the kitchen and cook dinner. I don't write a poem about it.

Audience Member: This is the United States of America which along with Western Europe was responsible in the twentieth century for most of the death, destruction, and starvation in the world. These countries are responsible for the rape of Latin America and Africa and Southeast Asia. Mr. Farah, I hope you enjoyed your stay here. These people don't want to talk about this.

(Long silence)

Nuruddin Farah: Well, thank you very much. I will continue replaying in my memory as I go back to Africa all the advice that has been given to me. And if I want to eat, I will remember to go into the kitchen and cook my own food. Thank you very much.

(Applause)

The Writer with a Politics

6 The Poetry of Witness

Carolyn Forché

■ I love politics but I think I love literature even more. I keep
thinking of today's theme according to a hierarchy that perhaps
might be illustrated by these lines in a poem of César Vallejo:
"Trust in the eyelid, not in the eye; in the step, never in the
stairs; in the wind and never in the bird." For some reason I saw
a classification there that appealed to me. Carolyn's task is to explain to us how these two things can merge rather than oppose.
This summer was a rather harrowing one because of the various
crises affecting not only Yugoslavia but Somalia and other places.
Possibly, because of her long experience of political activity,
Carolyn will be able to tell us better than anybody else how one
can bridge the gap between the private, poetic activity and a very
deep commitment to the betterment of one's world.

MARC CHÉNETIER, *Moderator*

The Poetry of Witness

I have been asked to address the subject of the writer *with* a
politics, and as I began preparing my remarks, it occurred
to me that one should, of course, clarify one's terms. What
is meant by the *writer*? I will speak today as a poet and oc-
casional essayist, with the understanding that my remarks do not per-
tain to any generalizable idea of "the writer," but only to particular
writers under specific conditions. The word *politics* presents more serious difficulties, particularly in the literary culture of the United
States, where the word is most often applied pejoratively, and where
politics is regarded as a contaminant of serious literary work. Our
poets, most especially, are relegated to the hermetic sphere of lyric
expressivity and linguistic art, where they are expected to remain un-
sullied by historical, political, and social forces. I speak to you today

135

as a rather contaminated poet, but my understanding of the political is in accord with Hannah Arendt's: "To be political, to live in a *polis* [means] that everything [is] decided through words and persuasion and not through force and violence. In Greek self-understanding, to force people by violence, to command rather than persuade, were pre-political ways to deal with people characteristic of life outside the *polis*." Finally, we are discussing the writer *with* a politics—and of this I can only say that it would be difficult for me to imagine a writer or intellectual who would profess to be without one. I live and write, however, in the administered world of a Western industrial state, where communicative thought and action are inhibited; where money circulates more fluently than verbal forms; where democracy does not extend beyond the scope of its institutions; where "total communication yields endless debate instead of change" (Otto Karl Werckmeister); in an economy so deeply dependent on military production that the national consciousness has been colonized by war; where armament and disarmament are simultaneously professed; where intellectuals find themselves "aesthetically oversensitized and politically numbed" (Werckmeister); and where the enlightened powerless occasionally produce works that are serendipitously drawn into political debates beyond the literary sphere. Fifteen years ago, while working as a human rights activist in El Salvador, I had the occasion to dine with a high-ranking officer in General Humberto Romero's military regime. The following aide-memoir was among the seven poems included in *The Country Between Us* that had to do with human rights in El Salvador.

THE COLONEL

WHAT YOU HAVE HEARD is true. I was in his house. His wife carried a tray of coffee and sugar, his daughter filed her nails, his son went out for the night. There were daily papers, pet dogs, a pistol on the cushion beside him. The moon swung bare on its black chord over the house. On the television was a cop show. It was in English. Broken bottles were embedded in the walls around the house, to scoop the kneecaps from a man's legs or cut his hands to lace. On the windows there were gratings like those in liquor stores. We had dinner: rack of lamb, good wine, a gold bell was on the table for calling the maid. The maid brought green mangoes, salt, a type of bread. I was asked how I enjoyed the country. There was a brief commercial in Spanish. His wife took everything away. There was some talk then of how difficult it had become to govern. The parrot said hello on the terrace. The colonel told it to shut up, and pushed himself from the table. My friend said to me with his eyes: say nothing. The colonel returned with a sack used to bring groceries home. He spilled many human ears on the table. They were like dried peach halves. There is no other way to say this. He took one of them in his hands, shook it in our faces, dropped it into a water glass. It came alive there. I am tired of fooling around, he said. As for the rights of anyone, tell your people they can go fuck themselves. He swept the ears to the floor with his arm and held the last of his wine in the air. Something for your poetry, no? he said. Some of the ears on the floor caught this scrap of his voice. Some of the ears on the floor were pressed to the ground.

San Salvador, May, 1978

In a book celebrated and maligned for extraliterary reasons, this was the most widely discussed and most controversial poem. North American audiences were curious to know whether the events narrated were "true." One critic theorized that I had stolen the central image from an Ernest Hemingway novel, in which bulls' ears were severed after a bullfight. The colonel's gross display of human bounty seemed unimaginably inappropriate in the context of a suburban dinner party, and yet I was credited with having invented this and other details out of whole cloth. An early essay which I wrote on the formation of the death squads in El Salvador piqued serious interest at the *New York Review of Books*, until its fact-checker learned from the U.S. Department of State that the death squads were a figment of this poet-fantast's unrestrained imagination. I had been beyond the borders of hegemonic reality long enough to have developed a serious delusional condition. In choosing to present truth in a literary form, I had transgressed literature and forfeited the credibility accorded to "objective" and institutionally constrained journalists.

In 1992, I returned to El Salvador for the first time in twelve years.

"Those who wanted you dead are dead, I was told. The colonel, too, is dead." While in the capital city, I met Doug Farrah, now of the *Washington Post.* "You're the poet who wrote the ears poem," he said. "Did you ever see my article in the *New York Times?*" I confessed that I hadn't. "It's about the ears, and the officer mentioned in the article was so proud of having his name in the *New York Times* that he had the article laminated for his wallet." In the library after my trip, I found the clipping from May 20, 1986:

SALVADORAN SOLDIERS TELL OF CUTTING OFF EARS OF DEAD REBELS.
Cerro Guacamaya, El Salvador (UPI)

Some Salvadoran soldiers say they have been cutting off the ears of dead leftist rebels to prove casualty counts. "We need something to prove we killed the terrorists," one sergeant said.

The officers of these soldiers say they are trying to end the practice, which they blame on the excitement of the moment.

Reporters traveling with an army unit on a counter-insurgency sweep in the northeastern province of Morazán on May 11 saw a soldier hold up two ears to prove that a guerrilla had been killed during a firefight near Cerro Guacamaya.

Other soldiers said it was not uncommon to cut the ears off the corpses of rebels to verify enemy casualties to commanders. But officers said they frown on the practice.

"Sometimes in battle, my men get excited and cut the ears off the dead terrorists," the lieutenant commanding the army unit said. "It is not something we order, but sometimes the excitement of the moment overcomes them."

As I read, it occurred to me to preserve the clipping myself, as a tangible fragment of that broken world. Perhaps it would one day serve some evidentiary purpose. Later in the trip, I was approached by an emissary from the American embassy, who informed me that I should stick to my poetry. "After all," he assured himself aloud, "nobody reads poetry."

During the past ten years, I have been collecting the work of poets from all over the world who endured conditions of social and historical extremity during the twentieth century—those who suffered wars, imprisonment, military occupation, house arrest, forced exile, and political repression. The result is an anthology of works in English and in translation, titled *Against Forgetting: Twentieth-Century Poetry of Witness*. The work is the result of a decade-long effort to understand the impress of such extremity upon the poetic imagination. My own journey began in 1980, upon my return from El Salvador, where I had worked for human rights, and led me through the occupied West Bank, Lebanon, and South Africa. Something happened along the way to the introspective poet I had been. My new work seemed controversial to some of my American contemporaries, who argued either against its "subject matter," or against my right as a North American to contemplate issues viewed as "foreign" to her work, or against any mixing of what they saw as the mutually exclusive realms of the poetic and the political. In attempting to come to terms with the question of poetry and politics, and seeking the solace of poetic camaraderie, I turned to Anna Akhmatova, Yannis Ritsos, Paul Celan, Federico García Lorca, Nazim Hikmet, and others. I began collecting their work, and soon found myself a repository of what began to be called "the poetry of witness." In thinking about these poems, I realized that the arguments regarding poetry and politics had been too narrowly defined. Regardless of apparent "subject matter," these poems bear the trace of extremity within them, and they are, as such, evidence of what occurred. They are also poems as much about poetry as are poems that have no subject other than poetry itself.

When I presented this collection to the publisher for consideration, I was asked what I meant by poets of witness—just what sort of poet would I include, and could I provide an example? I found myself telling the story of Miklós Radnóti.

In 1944, Miklós Radnóti, one of the foremost Hungarian poets of his generation, was sent to do forced labor in Yugoslavia. Once there, he was able to obtain a small notebook, in which he wrote his last ten poems, accompanied by a message in Hungarian, Croatian, German, French, and English: "[this] contains the poems of the

Hungarian poet Miklós Radnóti . . . to Mr. Gyula Ortutay, Budapest University lecturer. . . . Thank you in advance."

The Germans were losing the war and decided to evacuate the camp and return the workers to Hungary. Radnóti, guessing that the first column would be safest, volunteered to go back. The forced march he recorded in his poetry was arduous. Once in Hungary, he was placed in the hands of soldiers who, unable to find a hospital with room for these prisoners, and frightened of becoming absent without leave, took Radnóti and twenty-one others to a mass grave and executed them.

The pathos of this story is plain: Radnóti was killed for reasons of expedience. Moreover, if he had not volunteered to go back to Hungary, he might have been saved by Marshal Tito's partisans. But the story does not end—as millions of such stories ended—with an arbitrary execution and the anonymity of a mass grave. After the war, Radnóti's wife, Fani, was among those who found and exhumed the grave in the village of Abda. The coroner's report for corpse number 12 read:

> A visiting card with the name Dr. Miklós Radnóti printed on it. An ID card stating the mother's name as Ilona Grosz. Father's name illegible. Born in Budapest, May 5, 1909. Cause of death: shot in the nape. In the back pocket of the trousers a small notebook was found soaked in the fluids of the body and blackened by wet earth. This was cleaned and dried in the sun.

In the *Bori notesz* (Bor notebook) were Radnóti's final poems, among them the *Razglednici* (postcard poems) written during his imprisonment. They are collected in *Against Forgetting*, along with the works of one hundred and forty-four other significant poets, many of whom did not survive, but their works remain with us as poetic evidence of the dark times in which they lived. "There is a kind of writer appearing with greater and greater frequency among us who witnesses the crimes of his own government against himself and his countrymen," writes E. L. Doctorow, " . . . His is the universe of the imprisoned, the tortured, the disfigured, and doleful authority for the truth of his work is usually his own body. . . . So let us propose discussion of the idea that a new art, with its own rules, is being generated in the twentieth century: the Lieder of victims of the state." Most of the important poets of our century (particularly those not writing in English) can be included in their number.

This is a poetry that presents the American reader with an interesting interpretive problem. We are accustomed to rather easy categories: we distinguish between "personal" and "political" poems— the former calling to mind lyrics of love and emotional loss, the latter indicating a public partisanship that is considered divisive, even when necessary. The distinction between the personal and the political gives the political realm too much and too little scope: it renders the personal too important and not important enough. To globalize the feminist point that the personal is political is either to indicate that the personal is completely reducible to relations of power, or that the personal, on its own, can affect those relations and that power. There are dangers in both implications. The effacement of the personal can be seen not as a moment of real enlightenment, but as a surrender of the individual to the overbearing realities of an increasingly alienated world. If we give up the dimension of the personal, we risk relinquishing one of the most powerful sites of resistance. The celebration of the personal, however, can indicate a myopia, an inability to see how larger structures of the economy and the state circumscribe, if not determine, the fragile realm of individuality.

Radnóti's poems evade these easy categories. They are not just personal, nor are they, strictly speaking, political. What is one to make of the first lines of "Forced March":

> The man who, having collapsed, rises, takes steps, is insane;
> he'll move an ankle, a knee, an arrant mass of pain,
> and take to the road again

The poem becomes an apostrophe to a fellow marcher, and so it is not only a record of experience but an exhortation against despair. It is not a cry for sympathy but a call for strength. The hope that the poem relies on, however, is not "political" as such: it is not a celebration of solidarity in the name of a class or common enemy. It is not partisan in any accepted sense. It opposes the dream of future satisfaction to the reality of current pain. One could argue that it uses the promise of personal happiness against a politically induced misery, but it does so in the name of the poet's fellows, in the spirit of communality.

We need a third term, one that can describe the space between the institutions of political reproduction and the safe havens of the personal. I make this claim so that we can understand what so much of this century's poetry has been about. As Americans, we have been very lucky, wars for us (provided we are not combatants) are fought elsewhere, in other countries. The cities bombed are other people's cities. The houses destroyed are other people's houses. We are also fortunate in that we do not live under martial law; that there are nominal restrictions on state censorship; that our citizens are not forced into exile. I say all this not in the spirit of chauvinism, but to show the good fortune of our limitations, to indicate why it is that we can survive without a buffer zone between the individual and the state, why we can imagine ourselves (however misguided we might be in this) as individuals first and foremost. In the United States, we are legally and juridically free to choose our associates, and to determine our communal lives, but perhaps we should not consider our social lives as merely the products of our choice. The eighteenth-century founders of the United States understood that we live in a society that is constructed of interests and impulses: they imagined a sphere of public opinion and argument that was a free space between the comforts of the family and the institutions of the government. This public sphere was not to be part of the government but an influence upon it and a check on its powers and excesses. Thomas Jefferson claimed that with a free press, government might even become unnecessary. Such a belief in the strength of good arguments and in the suasive power of reason might seem hopelessly naive, but the demarcation of a space called "the social" (as we find it in the work of Hannah Arendt and Jürgen Habermas) can save us from the fatalism of claiming that all is ideology and the false promise of the dream of a pure subjectivity. The social is a place of resistance and struggle, where books are published, poems read, and protest disseminated. It is the sphere in which claims against the political order are made in the name of overt politics or less divisive forces of justice, and sometimes on behalf of such dangerous abstractions as "humanity."

By situating poetry in this social space, without, of course, relegating poetry to it, we can avoid some of our residual prejudices. A poem that calls on us from the other side of a situation of extremity cannot be judged by simplistic notions of "accuracy" or "truth to life." It will have to be judged, as Ludwig Wittgenstein said of confessions, by its consequences, not on our ability to verify its truth. In fact, the poem might be our only evidence that an event has occurred: it exists for us as the sole trace of an occurrence. As such, there will be nothing for us to base the poem on, no independent account that will tell us whether or not we can see a given text as being "objectively" true. Poem as trace, poem as evidence. Radnóti's final notebook entry, dated October 31, 1944, read:

> I fell beside him; his body turned over,
> already taut as a string about to snap.
> Shot in the nape. That's how you too will end,
> I whispered to myself; just lie quietly.
> Patience now flowers into death.
> *Der springt noch auf,* a voice said above me.
> On my ear, blood dried, mixed with filth.

This verse describes the death of his fellow prisoner, Miklós Lorsi, a violinist, and remains the only trace of his dying.

Such monstrosity has come to seem almost normal. It becomes easier to forget than to remember, and this forgetfulness becomes our spiritual remedy—a rejection of unnecessary sentimentality, a hardheaded acquiescence with "reality." Modernity, as Benjamin and Adorno argue, is marked by a superstitious worship of oppressive force and by a concomitant reliance on oblivion. Such forgetfulness, they argue, is willful and isolating: it drives wedges between the individual and the collective fate to which he or she is forced to submit. These poems will not permit us dis-eased complacency. They come to us with claims that have yet to be filled, as attempts to mark us as they have themselves been marked. They come together to form an anthological history of our age.

The poetry of witness reclaims the social from the political and in so doing defends the individual against illegitimate forms of compulsion. For too long, American literary criticism has sought to oppose "man" and "society," the individual against the communal, alterity against universality. Perhaps we can learn from the practice of these poets that these are not oppositions based on mutual exclusion but are rather dialectical complementaries that invoke and pass through each other. Extremity is born of the simplifying desire to split these dyads into separate parts. Extremity is the product of the drive to expunge one category in the name of another, to sacrifice the individual on the altar of the communal or vice versa. The poetry of witness is itself born in dialectical opposition to the extremity that has made such witness necessary. In the process, it restores the dynamic structure of dialectics. Because the poetry of witness marks the resistance to false attempts at unification, it will take many forms. It will be impassioned or ironic. It will speak in the language of the common man or in an esoteric language of paradox or literary privilege. It will curse and it will bless; it will blaspheme or ignore the holy. Its protest might rest on an odd grammatical inversion, a heady peroration to an audience, or on a bizarre flight of fancy. It can be partisan in a limited sense but is more often partisan in the best of senses, that is, it speaks for what might, with less than crippling irony be called "the party of humanity." I do not mean this in an unreflective way, as a celebration of some mythological "inherent" goodness in man's "innate" nature. Rather, I take the partisanship of humanity as a rejection of unwarranted pain inflicted on some humans by others, of illegitimate domination. I am guided in this by Hannah Arendt's meditation on the self-justifications of collaboration with oppression, on the claim that the resistance of the single individual does not count in the face of the annihilating superiority of totalitarian regimes that makes all resistance disappear into "holes of oblivion."

> The holes of oblivion do not exist. Nothing human is that perfect, and there are simply too many people in the world to make oblivion possible. One man will always be left alive to tell the story . . . the lesson of such stories is simple and within everybody's grasp. Politically speaking, it is that under conditions of terror, most people will comply but *some people will not*. . . . Humanly speaking, no more is required, and no more can reasonably be asked, for this planet to remain a place fit for human habitation. (Arendt 1977)

I would like to close with the expression of one final concern. In 1925, the French poet and philosopher Paul Valéry wrote about his fears that:

Our civilization is taking on . . . the structure and properties of a machine. . . . This machine will not tolerate less than world-wide rule; it will not allow a single human being to survive outside its control, uninvolved in its functioning. Furthermore, it cannot put up with ill-defined lives within its sphere of operation. Its precision, which is its essence, cannot endure vagueness or social caprice; irregular situations are incompatible with good running order. *It cannot put up with anyone whose duties and circumstances are not precisely specified.* It tends to eliminate those individuals who from its own point of view do not exactly fit, and to reclassify the rest without regard to the past or even the future of the species. . . . It has already begun to attack the ill-organized populations of the earth . . . decreeing that the highly organized must invariably take the offensive against the poorly organized. . . . The machine—that is, the Western World—could not help turning, one day, against those ill-defined and sometimes *incommensurable* men inside it. . . . So we are witnessing an attack on the indefinable mass by the will or the necessity for *definition.* Fiscal laws, economic laws, the regulation of labor, and, above all, the profound changes in general technology . . . everything is used for counting, assimilating, leveling, bracketing, and arranging that group of indefinables, those *natural solitaries* who constitute a part of the intellectual population. . . . It was never more than indirectly that society could afford the life of a poet, a thinker, an artist, whose works were unhurried and profound. (Valéry 1989)

The acceleration of the velocity of human experience is eroding our ability to sustain contemplation. The act of writing is not a means of expressing what is known but a means of recovering a knowledge otherwise irretrievable. "Writing plunges into the field of phrases, moving forward by means of adumbration, groping towards what it 'means' and never unaware, when it stops, that it's only suspending its exploration for a moment" (Jean-François Lyotard). We are living in a technological time that has so ingeniously managed to compress space that the velocity of experiential time has been increasing. Are there not regions of consciousness inaccessible at these speeds?

. . . as the new technologies [invade] public space and common time (invading them in the form of industrial objects of production and consumption, including "cultural" production and consumption), on a planetary scale, it is what we might call the most "intimate" space-time, in its most "elementary" syntheses, which is attacked, hounded and no doubt modified. (Bernard Steigler)

The future is negatively pre-empted; at the threshold to the 21st century outlines of a horror panorama begin to appear that shows general life interests to be endangered worldwide: the spiral of the arms race, the uncontrolled proliferation of nuclear weapons, the structural impoverishment of the developing countries, unemployment and growing social imbalances in the developed countries, problems of environmental impact, large-scale technologies operating at the risk of catastrophe—all of these provide the cues that have penetrated the public consciousness via the mass media. The intellectuals' answers reflect their helplessness no less than the politicians'. (Jürgen Habermas, 1985)

We are beginning to appreciate the destructive effects of our so-called progress upon an environment that we mysteriously persist in objectifying as somehow removed or separate from ourselves. But we have not yet begun to address how this destruction has altered us. Perhaps certain forms of human consciousness can also become extinct. The "unthinkable" was once a euphemism for human annihilation. Now that we have dubiously adjusted ourselves to thinking through and beyond this subject, perhaps the "unthinkable" can refer to all that can no longer be thought. In 1935, Valéry continued his argument: "The working conditions of the mind, have, in fact, suffered the same fate as all other human affairs, that is to say, they share in the intensity, the haste, the general acceleration of exchanges, as they do in all the consequences of the incoherence, the fantastic flickering of events." Fifty-seven years later, that "fantastic flickering" has brought into our living rooms such accelerated human developments that the world we now inhabit would have been unimaginable only a few years ago. The act of writing itself has become an act of resistance, and we must not only do everything in our power to protect that act, we must discover within ourselves and our collectivity, powers we never knew we had.

"If the hope of the world lies with human consciousness," writes President Vaclav Havel of Czechoslovakia, "then it is obvious that intellectuals cannot go on forever avoiding their share of responsibility for the world and hiding their distaste for politics under an alleged need to be independent."

The writer's life, the poet's life, is often solitary: hours of terror, moments of blissful evanescence, stolen time, absence, disguise, endurance of the anxiety of inner exile, and one's own lack of value to the larger society. Perhaps this society will not recognize us for our vigilance over creative thought, but with any effort and luck, we will preserve our capacity for future generations. Havel and others have reminded us that hope is not the same thing as optimism, and nowhere is hope deeper than in circumstances that seem most unpropitious.

Panel Discussion

Panelists: Eavan Boland, Marc Chénetier, Wayne Fields, Eric Pankey, Joe Pollack

Marc Chénetier: I don't want to go on in this Valérian mood in which the highly organized must take over against the poorly organized—but still, we need some organization. I would suggest that Carolyn bears witness to a double transgression: the transgression of the sheer literary and the transgression of what is expected of objective, journalistic reporting. This leads to a double loss of literariness and credibility. The incompatibility of the two modes seems to be lying at the center of her presentation. The "stick-to-your-poetry" remark is immediately answered with something that could be: "Don't meddle in politics." The accusation of being doubly foreign to the material at hand is one that answers in echo. You introduced a dichotomy between what you called poetry of the personal (I'm not certain that this is the only definition that could be given for the activity in question), and the public sphere. You suggested that there might be a need to find a third term to define this sort of activity. The idea we were being introduced to was a generic sort of dialectic but one that did not necessarily pose a central question that unites the two activities; and that is the linguistic activity. Between the writing as reaching, which you suggested was at the heart of the question in the words of Lyotard, and the poem as trace or evidence, there seems to be some tension. I'd like to turn to Eavan Boland as she has a wonderful title for one of her collections of poems, *Outside History*. Eavan, how do you see this tension between the personal and the public?

Eavan Boland: I go back next week to Ireland where every day ninety miles from my door individuals become victims of immense cruelty but also victims of anguish. Some of the points raised by Carolyn Forché touch on that. I want to put that question raised by Marc Chénetier about the dichotomy between the personal and the political into the context of a conference we had in Ireland last year, where Nuruddin Farah made some wonderful contributions and where Eastern European poets were a tremendous presence. They spoke about the difficulty for the poet when certain oppressive systems seem to become democratized. The poets are in the position of seeing their wishes as citizens being fulfilled but their identities as poets lost. In that polarity between the public and the personal, I have very strong feelings that the poet, or the writer, with a politics has to somehow align himself with a new identity in the democratized societies. This may well be happening. Mario Vargas Llosa spoke of having mixed feelings about the democratization of some parts of Latin America.

Now I'm a huge admirer of North American poetry, of Carolyn Forché's, of Eric Pankey's, and of others', but I'm very critical of the concept of the poet that is advanced in the English-speaking world. It seems to me that this idea of the poet, with the crucible of deciding whether you are a personal poet or a political poet, has become a withdrawn, self-regarding, self-congratulatory, and self-pitying concept. Poets like Radnóti, Celan, and Akhmatova suffered profoundly, but tyranny did not give them the attributes of poetry, it elicited from them the identity of poetry. If those poor souls who suffered so much and who witnessed the value of language could see what has happened to the concept of the poet in the English-speaking world, I think they would have the right to feel betrayed. Those poets did not ask of their value to a society. They died, in nothingness very often, with no sense of human value, let alone societal value. But they did not cease to witness language. They did not cease to put together and to heal that force fracture between the personal and the political in their work. If we read them, what we owe to them is to restate the identity of the poet. If we do not, we have no right to draw on the reality of their work without honoring the implication of it.

Eric Pankey: The concept of the poet in the United States is troubled because of capitalism and democratization. We've produced something that even we, the producers of it, don't see as a commodity or valued. Yet we go on doing it. I believe we honor the art, the way Eavan might insist that we do, by continuing to do it. I would like to consider this notion of what Carolyn called the political realm, where all is decided through words and persuasion, and not through force. One practicing poetry would like to believe that that, too, is the realm of poetry, but unfortunately the example that we see in our country is that the political does not behave that way; it behaves with deception, lies, misinformation, and innuendo. I cannot speak for all poets from the United States, I can speak as one poet, who happens to be a white man, who happens to be part of the dominant tradition in American poetry. Let me say what I think poetry, under all labels, attempts to do. It's no match for the political, because the political has made its mind up. What poetry is, and has been, is speculative; it is a mode in which we investigate and attempt to reach something that I would call the spiritual. The spiritual is what the safe poets in North America share with those who are threatened elsewhere. The beautiful to the politicians is of no use unless it's in the acquisition of power. Poetry is about hope. I think that most of us who participate in this activity, the making of poems, have a hope that through speaking, we will come to something that might be recognized as the truth, that might utter something against domination, control, brutality. The subtle lies of politics share little with the subtle truths of poetry.

The purpose of poetry is not power; it is, as Carolyn said, to bear witness. I come from a religious background where people would stand up in the front of the church and do something they called testifying, where they would get up and tell you all of their sins.

There was something questionable about that behavior, because what was most interesting were the sins, not the end where they say I'm forgiven. What I'm hoping that poetry can do by testifying is ask for relief, for forgiveness. Listening to the discussion yesterday, I wanted the writers speaking to tell us what we could do as writers, and as citizens, to affect change in Somalia, to save that country. I don't know what I can do as a poet. I know what I can do as a citizen. But I don't know what I can do as a poet.

Marc Chénetier: Joe Pollack, as a journalist, do you think that poetry will necessarily betray the required objectivity that characterizes your trade? Is there room for this sort of testimony from a journalist's viewpoint?

Joe Pollack: I think there's a great deal of room for it. As a journalist and a writer, I think that there is certainly an area of working together in confirming the poetry of witness or providing information that would make the poetry of witness possible. I think of Carolyn speaking about the reporter Doug Farrah. Her accuracy and her truth were questioned in the ears poem. It was the journalist who was able to serve as a witness and to speak to the truth of it. In the areas where I work, for example, in the arts, theatre, and film, I'm a writer with a politics, as are playwrights, for example. It is important to make sure that their writings about politics or their writings involving politics, are looked at, analyzed, and made to stand, to affect other people. There are plays such as *Death and the Maiden* about Chile or Caryl Churchill's *Mad Forest* about the revolution in Romania. It is the function of the critic to help the writer put forth the politics and to protect it—to protect its presence in the world.

Marc Chénetier: Wayne, when it comes to a writer like Ezra Pound, who mixes his poetry with a certain type of politics or when Wyndham Lewis does that, will the introduction of such politics, the introduction of any politics in the poetry necessarily ruin it?

Wayne Fields: I am a reader first and foremost, and a teacher of readers, so I think about these issues in a sort of skewed fashion from the subject of the conference. The problem for me as a reader in those contexts is largely a problem of authority. The newspaper version of

"The Colonel" was told in lifeless, unrealistic prose: "Sometimes in battle men get excited and cut off the ears of dead terrorists." This language explains how it could be true in a clinical, dispassionate way, in which the ears are real but the dead terrorists are not. The men who get excited have feeling, but the dead terrorist does not. It strikes me as incredible that this article was needed to confirm the situation. For me, it had been only too real before. I suppose the general resistance to a poem like "The Colonel" is because we know it's true, not because we suspect it's false.

When you have a writer whose poetry has a kind of authority but whose politics lacks that authority, it creates a problem for me as a reader, one that never gets resolved. As a teacher, I cannot ignore Pound although I do so as much as possible when it's a problematic context, or I try to apologize that I'm treating the poetry the way I am. In the case of Pound, there is a collision between these two authorities. It seems to me that Pound's politics is at crucial moments exposed as false by his aesthetics. When he is at his truest moment a poet, he doesn't need anyone else to stand in judgment of his politics. His own language does it.

Marc Chénetier: Carolyn, do you have the feeling that this collision of authorities that Wayne was talking about is problematic—does the political undermine the poetic authority?

Carolyn Forché: I agree with him about Pound being judged by his own language. Thank you for noticing the language in the journalistic piece. It might be true that the poem was resisted because people didn't want to believe it. It seemed rather threatening. But I want to clarify a few things. I think that all poetry and writing can be read politically. I wish politics were more literary. The problem that we have in the United States is that our own politics and our own ideology are invisible to us. What we call political is what has been made visible by its oppositional nature. So we accuse those of being political who expose us to a different way of thinking. That is why black poets are accused pejoratively of writing politically as are Hispanic-American poets and Native American poets. That is why we have "feminist poets" as opposed to "real poets." All language is political. Politics can be read in what the language leaves out, or the worlds the language leaves out, as much as it can be read in what the language makes explicit.

I resist this notion of poetry of spirituality and beauty a bit. I don't think my poems can any longer be about the beautiful or even about hope. I want to share with you what Paul Celan said in Bremen in 1958. He said—and Celan was a survivor of the Holocaust until he committed suicide—"Poetry can no longer speak the language which many a willing ear seems to expect from it. Its language has become more austere and factual. It distrusts the beautiful and it attempts to be true. It is thus a grayer language—a language which among other things wants to see its musicality situated in a region where it has nothing in common with that harmoniousness which in a more or less unconcerned manner sounded with and alongside the horrors." I have a feeling that one's poetry is changed by these circumstances. In the *Poetry of Witness,* I wanted to argue that these works were not less poetic because they had a subject matter and were naively representational. I wanted to argue that rather than reading these poems as representational, we can read them as evidence of the wound—as what happened to the language when these things happened to the poet and the poet's world. This is what I think Nuruddin Farah was saying yesterday when he talked about what is happening to him as a writer as Somalia dies.

I want to thank Eavan Boland for illuminating for us that very important idea of the way we conceive of ourselves. I get uncomfortable when poets and writers complain about not being important in their culture and start talking enviously about poets who are tortured or imprisoned as an indication that they are being taken seriously. I don't want to be tortured and put into prison to be taken seriously. I don't think that we should think of ourselves as mattering that much. The work is what should matter. We should be worried about the fact that we still have this illusion that we're living in separate countries that have nothing to do with each other or each other's realities, and that we are not part of what is happening in Somalia and South Africa. I think that it's very easy here to miss what's going on in the rest of the world. It takes a great deal of research and effort to stay informed.

Marc Chénetier: Mallarmé said that if you want to be a poet, please write in other ways than the newspapers. If you turn to a political organizer you want to collaborate with and say, "Hi, I'm a poet," isn't the immediate reaction, "Oh, just another damn poet"? What is the status of the poet when he enters politics? Did you ever see it as an obstacle?

Carolyn Forché: No.

Marc Chénetier: In your own political life, Eavan, is your status as a poet something that tends to repel the ordinary militant?

Eavan Boland: I want to be clear about the question. When you say the ordinary militant, the ordinary militant in our country is a fairly formidable creature and if you mean—

Marc Chénetier: I mean the nonpoet.

Eavan Boland: I think there needs to be a distinction made between the poetry that preceded literacy or survived nonliteracy, as in Ireland, and the rise of poetry, however wonderful, in a country that is coincident with the rise of literacy. In Ireland, the eighteenth-century punitive laws by the British government seriously affected literacy in the Catholic peoples in Ireland who could not go to school under those laws. Therefore there was a strong identification of the survival of poetry in a nonliterate situation. I would not want to glamorize it, because Bardic poetry was in fact a very sophisticated and sometimes arid poetry. In the Slieve Luachra and North Kerry regions of Ireland, people could remember an enormous amount of poetry. They were not poets, and they were not readers, they were the carriers of poetry. Now, the status of a poet is clearer in a community where there has been an identity between the voicelessness and powerlessness of a people and the survival of their consciousness in the poetic forms. There are enormous tensions in Ireland between the poet and the community, and between the poet and militant factions, such as members of the Irish Republican Army, who profess enormous literary interest on almost all occasions and who write books, but who have savage intentions toward literature, I believe. In the United States there has been a rise of a wonderful literature coincident with the rise of literacy. Therefore it genuinely makes it more difficult for the relationship between the poet and community to be clarified along that edge.

Carolyn Forché: It was in Salvador that I was taught to value poetry, not in my own country. When I was there I at first didn't tell anyone I was a poet, because all the human rights workers were mostly international human rights lawyers or something like that. I wasn't accustomed to functioning in the world of bureaucracy. My work took place on the ground; it was very physical work. There was one night when we were all very afraid so we began talking about ourselves, which people don't generally do unless they are feeling that it might be their last opportunity to talk. They asked me what I did, and I told them I was just a poet. They were furious with me for saying that I was "just" a poet. They said—I think because they had a pre-literate and oral literary culture—"That is what has kept us alive when we go into prison, poetry is what we memorize and hold in our hearts, poetry is the strength of our language. Who taught you that it wasn't important?" So I tried to explain in my fumbling way what had taught me this, how I had learned that poetry wasn't important. When I came back to the United States, I thought, "Well, the most important thing now will be to keep this distinction in mind, that poetry is deeply important but that I should never merge that with any sense of inflated self-importance of the poet."

Marc Chénetier: There seems to be some consensus, even when there were premises of tensions between your view and Eric's, that after all, we believe that poetry is the longest-lived resistance movement in the history of the world. When it does coincide with a tradition, it is extraordinarily powerful, and even when it doesn't coincide it is still essential to preserve.

Eric Pankey: I can remember the first time I read "The Colonel." The two feelings I had were horror and hope. I thought to myself that this is the truth. We had all been hearing that there were death squads. The poem seemed to make it real, and it made it real for the people that I was with at the time. It was not an article in the *New York Times*, it was poetry by Carolyn Forché that did that. When I say that the purpose of poetry is hope, it is that it dares to speak, and it dares to give shape to something that could be lost. By hope

I mean that the truth stays with us, that we will not be allowed to forget, that we will not have to suffer these groups coming onto our campus and saying, for instance, that the Holocaust did not occur, because there is evidence, there are poems, there are stories. I think that poetry, no matter how fragmented, no matter how its language is changed by our modern condition, is still attempting wholeness.

Marc Chénetier: I would like your reaction, Carolyn. (Excuse me for being so Eurocentric, but I'm not only Eurocentric and Eurocentered, I'm just Euro, period.) There was this Belgian writer, wonderful writer, by the name of Conrad Detrez, who died a few years ago, and he used to say, "I want poetry and literature to do musical painting for me; for the rest I have a telephone." How would you react to that? Is this irresponsible in your view?

Carolyn Forché: Musical painting is a rather nice metaphor, just as architecture as frozen music is a nice one. Some people think literature is an escape, that they can stay away from everything and live in an egg of gold and light and language and the past. It's not possible to stay separate, it's only an illusion that one is separate. It's an illusion that we labor to maintain. I don't agree with him. I think his statement is essentially deeply political—"for the rest I have the telephone"—and he didn't know it. He was violating his own dictum, I think.

Marc Chénetier: All right, we're on an edge here, so it's a good place to jump from.

Audience Member (Nuruddin Farah): I come from Somalia, which is a country known for its oral tradition. It's one of the few countries I know where, if there are six persons sitting in a room and a poet walks in, the poet will be given six chairs. Everyone out of respect will give their chair to the poet. There is nowhere that I know that poets are revered as much as they are in Somalia. But the tragedy of Somalia is also that at least fifteen to twenty poets have either died or are on the point of death or starvation. So this is the reason why the idea of linking a country through its poetry, though its literature, becomes quite important, and the reason is because the poet, as you have said, is the carrier, the repository of the people's memory. The poet is the one who has survived the condition of oral literature and then continues defying all other forms of activity in order to continue carrying the flag. The poet becomes that humanity and the death of that poet is the death of that humanity.

Audience Member: I would like to comment first on what you said about the telephone and to what Nuruddin just said about the death of a poet. It seems to me—I don't write poetry myself, I read it—that poetry is informed by what is happening in the present, but the reason it endures is because it is speaking to us on a deeper level. When your poet made the comment about the telephone, well, that's fine for what's going on in the present, but poetry is working with us on a much deeper level. That's why it endures and why in an oral tradition the people will keep it with them. When you say the death of the poet is the death of a humanity, I don't think it's the death of the poet, which is what Carolyn and Eavan were also saying, but the death of the poetry. It isn't the poet that becomes the humanity but the poetry itself that sustains humanity.

Audience Member: We have talked about the role of the poet or author in relation to politics, but it seems that we have an image of political activity that is not very realistic. Political activity as a specialized area of activity is a misguided concept that exists in most societies in the world right now. Any person in any walk of life is political. A doctor in his own position can act in a way to change the situation in which he's working or to concede or compromise or accept the situation in which he's working. In literature and in politics if we give the field to a specialist it will be our downfall. In all literature and in all art, the nature of the activity is such that it is not production for profit. It is creativity just for the sake of it. Any literary activity by nature is political because it is opposing the existing political system, proposing a different kind of activity, a different definition of work. I was a university lecturer in Iran, and I discovered that it was impossible to teach D. H. Lawrence to a sexually segregated class. It defeats the purpose. But I didn't choose to be political; the situation was political. Ever since that happened, I find I'm a great lover of American literature, but I find a lot of the current literature to be self-indulgent. It's like a suburban household. It is political, of course. It is making a political statement about the frame of mind of the writer. But it is impotent. It is decadent.

Marc Chénetier: There was a very interesting comment you made a while ago, Carolyn, about poetry moving away from representation and being evidence of the wound, which I really loved as a definition of the impact of politics on poetry. There is the other view of this that has been traditionally promoted, particularly in societies that are profoundly imbued with an oral tradition: that is, poetry as healing, or as community healing. Wayne, do you see this as a possibility today?

Wayne Fields: I have this double interest in literature and politics; most people tend to think that I'm dealing with opposites. Somehow for me my attraction to both of them is the same, that they are both about longing, they are both deeply personal to me. The idea that there could be a poetry that was not personal and a politics that wasn't personal is conceivable to me for somebody else, but it's not true for me. There are times when I think of the state as a version of myself and there are times when I think of myself as a version of the state—with all the barbaric tendencies and special interests that are represented there. I think that we are driven to both, after a longing, after what you called healing, what I call wholeness, some kind of completion. I liked the image that kept coming up of giving voice to those tendencies and interests that somebody else was trying to have us lose, trying to annihilate from memory as from fact; that there is this constant effort in poetry to restore the community by linking the reader and the text to the writer and to all those other elements that are a part of that community. That is where, for me, the political urge comes from in the first place. These aren't antithetical things that I'm committed to, they reflect the same kind of longing and the same kind of need both in my larger, social life, if I can make that distinction, and to me personally. To dichotomize the two is misleading. The end for both, the passion for both, has to do with my resistance and my longing for wholeness.

Marc Chénetier: Since most people here would agree that any writing is of necessity political, I was tempted to think it would be nice if we could turn it around and see that everything becomes poetical. Is that too farfetched?

Audience Member (Writer Michael Castro): I agree that poetry is spiritual in nature. I think that the responsibility of the poet is to write about what we know about our own and the human spirit. It's very dangerous to buy into the separation between spirit and world that is really at the heart of Western culture. So personally, I write poems about things that move me, which can be very insular, hermetic things and also things that are very removed in a geographical sense. Whitman said, "I am man, I suffered, and I was there." And he wasn't there. But the point is that he was connected to what we might call Big Mind. He did not live in Little Mind. So I think it's very dangerous if we capitulate to the definition of what we can or can't do, that we have to look at the views of literary editors, critics, and the media for those who will take us seriously. I think that ultimately we define the limits or limitlessness of our art. I think there is ground for hope rather than despair. I think this event is one witness to that. If one samples widely the poetry that is being written today in the United States, not all of it is as decadent as you describe. Unfortunately, many of the poets who share the concerns and interests of the truly world-class artists we've been exposed to in this conference are more marginalized. Nevertheless, they do get their poems heard. Many of them don't even concern themselves with publishing their poems. If you go to readings, which spring up in this community virtually every day of the month, and sample what's written, some of which is very bad as poetry and some of which is very good, a great deal of it speaks to what concerns people in our culture. That is what's going on in the United States, the frustrations that citizens feel in the face of the government's activities and the larger concern for the condition of the spirit on the planet Earth. Ultimately this tide will rise and will define what is legitimate as poetry.

Carolyn Forché: I get a little uncomfortable when we focus, especially North Americans, on guilt, because that allows the story to be about ourselves and our own feelings. I know that sounds sacrilegious in our culture, particularly in the 1990s, but let me try to explain. I've been working for the last few years with Holocaust scholars and with people who videotape survivors to preserve the story. The videotapes are in the Fortunoff collection at Yale University. One of the things that the Holocaust scholars have imparted to me is a distrust of redemption, that the poetry and literature that come out of the Holocaust, while it can be read as a document of the Holocaust and a literary work, particularly in the case of a poet as great as Paul Celan, will become a comfort that certain people survived and wrote, that this writing exists, and that there is a quality of redemption in the very fact that this writing can live despite this horrible atrocity.

Newspaper reporters, with all due respect to the profession, refer to their work as "covering." They cover wars or political situations. Healers may think metaphorically of bandaging. But I wish we weren't so worried about healing, because keeping the wound open allows people to feel truth is being told. What are we trying not to see?

When I was in Beirut we were in a little place trying to eat dinner and there was a lot of shelling in the district. It became dark so we brought out candles. Everyone was trying to speak calmly about things besides the shelling. One American said, "I just want it to happen fast. I just want the shell to hit dead center in this table, and I want to die without knowing anything." One of the Beirut women turned to her and said, "That's so American. You don't want even to feel your own death." We all laughed and everyone was relieved, but I think that we who have suffered least should be least concerned about healing ourselves and our psychic wounds. I think that we need to see them, feel them, hold them open, understand them and try not to feel better. The work is not about how we feel. Hope is not really necessary. Monsignor Romero told me that in El Salvador. He said, "Don't worry about hope. You don't have to hope. In fact, if you hope you're in big trouble because then you're courting despair, the other side. If you despair you'll give up and stop working and doing things for human rights. You'll become depressed and then where will we be? Just forget about hope. Keep marching, one foot in front of the other, and do the moral act in every moment you're living. Don't worry about whether you're feeling good or safe or healed or happy." I know I'm blaspheming my contemporary culture so I'll stop.

(Applause)

Marc Chénetier: This is awful! Joe?

Joe Pollack: I applaud that because I think that's the job of everybody who writes—poet, essayist, novelist, or newspaper writer. It's an important part of the job to keep that open, so people keep seeing what is wrong.

Audience Member (Writer Michael Castro): I have a question for Joe Pollack. Is the *St. Louis Post-Dispatch* covering this conference? Why is it that the *Post* never covers poetry readings and other events where significant writers come in and talk in our community?

Joe Pollack: I've got to some extent duck the question. I think that we cover a lot of writers. Perhaps we don't cover enough, but those are decisions that I don't make. There are editors and executives who make those decisions about general coverage. Sorry.

Audience Member (Jonathan Smith): I would like to speak as a marginalized American poet. I think we've all pretty much agreed that poetry, writing, and politics have a connection. As a marginalized voice, I have experienced the American tradition and culture as something much different from perhaps Eric and Carolyn's. Eric mentioned his religious tradition of testifying. My religious tradition of testifying may look the same but is in fact completely different. People stand up in front of the church and say things, but the things they say and how they respond are different. I imagine I would feel out of place in Eric's religious tradition, and he would probably feel the same in mine. My idea of what a poet should do and what I do as a poet suggest to me that Eric and I live in two very different worlds. Our poetry reflects those things.

One thing that has not come up is rap music, whether it's music or poetry or politics. I think we might be able to make a legitimate argument that rap is poetry. One reason the *St. Louis Post-Dispatch* doesn't cover an event such as this is that if 2 Live Crew were here, there would be no place to sit. In terms of politics, in rap particularly, those poets are doing something that perhaps we should be doing.

Eavan Boland: I think you bring up interesting points. I'll respond to them as an outsider. It is absolutely true that this auditorium would be filled by any contemporary rock musician. If that were the judgment of poetry then people like Celan and Akhmatova are irrelevant. There was nobody there when they died. They were of no importance, visibly, at that moment. The judgment of the value of the work of art is totally unrelated to the numbers attending, to the audience reception. If that were not true then Kafka and Joyce and these people would be snuffed out.

The interesting question about rap music threw me. There is a difference between self-expression and art. You have the duty as an artist to maintain it and to state it. But there is no art without self-expression. I would be very easily persuaded that rap is a very powerful and important part of self-expression. I know that rap is formed from a community voice; it doesn't surprise me that you have a very powerful constituency attending it. I would be open to the argument that there is art within the self-expression in rap music, but it wouldn't depend upon how many numbers were there. It would depend on the private impulses within the statement.

Marc Chénetier: There is time for one more question. Randolph?

Audience Member (Randolph Pope): Certainly I prefer moral poetry, and I've been very moved by what Carolyn said, but let me put a word in for immorality in poetry. I think that we have dealt very lightly with Ezra Pound and with other writers who show us the dark side of ourselves—singing the beauty of the SS soldiers, for example. It is the outsider who reaches out to us, the one who speaks about the horror of that which we cannot understand. In the same way, I think that Carolyn's poem works for other people and for us. I think that Georg Trakl, a very misguided German poet, for example, is one who shows us this horrifying side. Some of the oral poets have sung of destruction and violence. The Serbs have a great tradition of oral poetry that has served to strengthen their nationalism and to extol acts of violence. Poetry also does this, it cuts ears, and it also makes us understand why this is done. Perhaps eventually immorality can also be moral.

Marc Chénetier: I think it would be lovely if we could close on this reopening of the opening paradoxes and do what all good poetry should do, and that is to invite us towards the open. On this I propose we close this session.

7   Cold Turkey

Breyten Breytenbach

■ Our speaker this afternoon has for a long time, and I'm
sure quite against his will, been an emblem of opposition to
the South African regime and its discriminatory policies. And
not simply because he spent so many years in jail, in solitary
confinement, or because of his interracial marriage, but because
of his stirring, courageous, and always other-than-self-serving
books, most particularly, *The True Confessions of an Albino
Terrorist*. As a poet, a memoirist, a storyteller, an accomplished
painter, he has spent his life in the center of our subject. And
he, incidentally, invents titles like no other. My favorite: *In
Africa Even the Flies Are Happy*. Breyten Breytenbach.

WILLIAM H. GASS, *Moderator*

Cold Turkey

This is going to be the last session, so I'm in a lucky and
difficult position: lucky because, as we say, *hy wat laaste
lag, lag de lekkerste* (he who laughs last, laughs the
most); daunting, because I have to follow in the foot-
steps of those who came before me, particularly after having listened
to that very profound poem this morning, because I consider Carolyn's whole paper as having been one long poem. Coming last means
that I've also been able to pick up on some of your ideas, so don't
be upset, you other contributors, if you find I've stolen some of your
best phrases. That's also part of being a writer.

I entitled my paper "Cold Turkey," because what I had in mind
was to present to you, perhaps shamefacedly, the manifestation or the
spectacle of some shudders of withdrawal from the addiction of believing that human nature could be changed for the better. But the
paper turned out to be slightly different, I think, as you will hear.

162

Obviously the title, or at least the theme within which we are going to be working this afternoon, is "The Writer with a Politics." I feel that justifies me in making rather broad sweeping statements, very abrupt pronouncements, and perhaps very unreasoned and provocative ones. After all, it's the *writer* with politics. We assume the writer could be somewhat of a dreamer. He or she is a writer first, not a politician who's been stricken with writing. Before getting to the paper I'm going to read this poem, although it's one I should read at the end. It ends with the words *hamba kahle!* which is Zulu for "go well." It's a greeting which you extend when people leave, but it's also used metaphorically at the grave's edge, *hamba kahle,* go well. The title is "For Françooi Viljoen."

> there are things one never forgets oh dissemblers—
> cat's paws of darkness over closed eyelids
> the brief clear gaping of the bullet's cough
> car headlamps slitting the night to ribbons
> painted white masks of the buffoon and the whore
> the hangman's laughter like a dose of strychnine
> the flesh-colored flame
> satin purse that cannot scorch the
> black rooks on red haystacks
> a dwarf with a whistle on the elephant's back
> the tower filled since years with whispering fire
> the green swollen booming of the sea
> the long broken downhill shuffle of old age
> braking till it's worn to the knees—
> these, the inalienable souvenirs
> the heart's tiny mirrors lugged the length of the journey
>
> we all walk that road
> of life on its way to death—
> murderers, burglars, drug addicts and firebugs
> thugs, embezzlers, rapists
> and fellow terrorists—
> you like I tattooed in lineament and skin
> single in our destiny—
> till we climb through the gap
> into the kitchen pantry

and the earth munches us to the bone
—'finished; dispatched; cracked; home'—

go well friends by the light of the body
go well marked by what's never forgotten
to the final prison where all memory goes dark—
hamba kahle!

(Breytenbach 1988)

A word of excuse to my fellow panelists. I only was able to let you have a copy this morning of what I've prepared. It's handwritten. It was to stop you from working out your arguments too long in advance, Nuruddin.

Cold Turkey

(Being shudders of withdrawal from the addiction of believing that human nature could be ameliorated or human behavior changed for the better)

To say "The Writer and Politics" is to evoke a quandary. We hear the din of distant battles and through the smoke we may still read shifting lines of opposition and collaboration, treachery and foolhardiness. There's a pungency on the air, of burnt books and scorched flesh, and sometimes we come across the remnants of ideas and fermenting corpses like so many discarded arguments. Let us, provisionally, see politics embodied as State, Party, Faith, or even just the Correct Consciousness. Then we can trace throughout history and in all cultures the story of the fatal attraction between public power and writing. Only too often the writers who became ensnared in the incestuous relationship could only survive once they gave up the struggle for justice to become politicians, or court orderlies, or believers. Either way it would seem to have been, and remain, a no-win position: the apostates were exiled from the areas of shared experience, the social strategists ended up as political cannon fodder.

An ample crop of theories could naturally be harvested from attempts to circumscribe the interaction between writing and politics, from the description of how they use the same tools. A sharing detrimental to writing, I may add, which usually only has a lexicon of dead words and a clutch of contaminated dreams to show for its involvement with politics.

What are the shared premises and operation modes? Can it be the manipulation of power? The creation of perceptions? Exploiting the links and the breaks between reality and illusion? The sharpening or the effacement (even the disfiguration) of the features of consciousness? To engender conscience? Moving cynicism from apathy to active service? Do the two forms of public engagement really labor the void in similar fashion? Doesn't writing also aim to be situated, as politics projects itself to be, at the heart of life while holding out the hope of going beyond to an enhanced existence?

And can one reasonably hope to contribute any fresh insights to that which has already been observed? If I persist in seeing them as entities of an equation pulling and pushing over a changing field of shared concerns, in what way did our times modify the meshing? I can only hope to step over the battlefield of stale abstractions by linking my remarks to a personal, quirky, and perhaps perverse trajectory; to explain how this pilgrim progressed from the never-never land of promise to my present location of nowhere.

For me, more and more, writing is about traveling and not about destinations. Identity is a passing creation, the sum of positions gained and evacuated during the trip. (I use "gained" and "evacuated" here as Gallicisms.) To be, it is normally assumed, one has to define, in some form of mental defecation, the social, political, or cultural group you identify with. At the moment, if I'm not mistaken, I have no recognizable politics in the accepted sense. But this is not the same as being in a no-go zone.

Obviously—and at the risk of contradicting the distance or the abdication just penned out—I still adhere to a body of values: I remain partial and partisan; I insist upon making choices and acting accordingly, in speaking a mind as uncluttered as I can make it. I also try to be aware of the implications and the consequences of my rambling.

The poet with a politics must come across as rather naive, abrupt in her or his judgments, somewhat of a dreamer. After all, he or she is not a politician stricken by spasms of writing, but a writer first offering (for example) the poem as the potential survivor of the act of death at the moment of writing. Thinking like this on one's hind legs furthermore makes for a format of cut-and-dried statements encapsulating arbitrary reasoning.

Even so, and in order to advance, I'd itemize some of the values of left and right as follows. On the left one would expect to encounter: the importance ascribed to the creative powers of imagination; the concept that every action has a political significance; that economic forces should be politically accompanied for social purposes; that internationalism is a virtue and third-worldism a well-understood obligation; that deciphering the world is a complicated and open-minded but unavoidable process; that disagreeing with received truths is a necessary survival technique; that utopias must be created just out of reach to keep us on our toes, but that realizing any such utopia will be an unmasking of death; that knowledge should be a transmission of the means to power to people thus enabling them to take part in their own destinies; that nationalism and the prioritization of ethnicity are seizures of the collective mind bringing about generalized stupidity; that any configuration of society ought to be open and tolerant and responsive to spontaneity; that, to quote Blake, "When the Reverence of Government is lost, it is better than when it is found."

On the right then, there would be: aggressive or nostalgic nationalism, also called patriotism; the desirability of individual fulfillment as highest achievement; consensus politics; leaving economics to the experts; the coddling of minority rights and the extreme unction of affirmative action; virtual reality; politically correct thinking; Eurocentrism; confusing power with right (as in, "if I can afford to buy it I have the right to do so"); pragmatism (as in the integration of the attitude that there's not enough for everybody on this planet, so let us save the strong); charity; ethnic art; liberating the media from the dead weight of message; the premise that there is no link between cause and effect except as in the case of investment and profit; beautiful bodies; safe sex; ecology; democracy.

I'm tempted to stretch even further the tenuous line of my thinking. To the left, revolution; to the right, politics. Because revolution is a negation of "the art of the possible" whereas politics is the arcane craft of disempowering the population. To the left, people as humans; to the right, "the people" as masses, and elites. To the left, associations forming civil society; to the right, cabals, expert committees, vigilantes, brotherhoods, the Vanguard Party, the State with its no-menklatura. To the left, understanding or confusion; to the right "correct" understanding, or indifference. To the left, the Way; to the right, the Truth. To the right, banks and the IMF, Muslim fundamentalists, Switzerland, the security establishment and all manner of political police and informers and pimps, arms dealers, the radical chic, cultural workers, the USA, the New World Order, freedom fighter leaders, caviar socialists, postmodernism, Billy Graham, the North, the Pope, Czar Leonid Yeltsin the First. To the right also the invidious choice presented as: vote for me, my party may be bad but that of our opponents is even more horrible. To the right, similarly, the Stalinist premise that one must keep (to) the ranks of discipline when faced by a common enemy. (In South Africa, incidentally, this imprecation translates as "One settler, one bullet," or "No education before liberation.") To the left, the fumbling search for justice; to the right, intervention by power players in the name of human rights.

The politics you practice is one way of impacting upon the world in which you live; it is also part of the spectrum through which that world impinges upon your awareness. This dialectic brings to mind a story I was told years ago by Beauford Delaney, an American painter who lived in Paris. Beauford's great-grandmother had been born before the disappearance of slavery. An old gentleman she knew, let's call him Freedom for argument's sake, used to be the property of a one-legged slave-holder. Whenever the owner bought new shoes he would pass one, the left one for which he had no need, on to Freedom. Freedom would wait until he had two "new" left shoes before donning them as a pair. By the end of his life, Freedom, who'd started off with two perfectly normal feet, hobbled along on a crippled right clubfoot. When Beauford told this tale his body would shake and tears would roll down his cheeks.

We live in extraordinary times, confronted by a rapidly shifting series of momentous events, buffeted by false hopes, but also brought face to face with unpalatable disillusions. The horrors we witness, and which we seemingly can do nothing about, have broken the back of our capacity for outrage. As lounge animals we sit there, flooded by global information and the immediate deceptions of trivialization. We are neither called upon to invest an effort at understanding nor to participate in the digestion of communication, and we have our impotence shoved down our throats. The need for survival oblivion has reduced our languages to advertisement jingles, smoothing the texture of our means of perception. We transferred our memories to data bases and are losing the transformative art of remembering. Even our inventiveness is now being defined by the format of sound bites and the contours of computer programs. Our imaginations are ever more sky-lined by the hysterical and narcissistic cry for live-time novelty. We have all sorts of festering answers to questions that can no longer be asked. We don't even get drunk anymore. Is that which we perceive reality or lie? Suddenly there is nowhere to look forward to and nothing to be nostalgic about.

One of the fond conceits that I grew up with was that writers were intelligent people. (One of the biggest mistakes is the belief that writing ought to be a game of intelligence.) And, because they were so often the critics of an existing order, I furthermore took the politically conscious writers to be fired with a refined sense of ethical awareness.

Now I know it is more complicated. Writers, blinded perhaps by the assumed influence of their insights and flattered by the shadow of power, are often the last to read the times, to recognize the failure of their pompous dreams, to decode the manipulation of words and the juggling of ideas in the fruit machines of perceptions. We do not see how crippled we are by the fact of being parlor guests in the mansions of the rich. We cajole and vie for acceptance. We all want to be liked and stroked for making sense.

Seldom are writers summoned to shoulder responsibility for the false routes they enticed so many people to embark upon. In Europe, for instance, a generation of writing thinkers, sad television donkeys really, have progressed from the pious left of pie in the sky to the abrasive right without, apparently, sacrificing any credibility or self-assurance. So that where we once had these public consciences writing and marching against imperialist wars in Vietnam or colonialist repression, or simply concerned about the hounding of "illegal" immigrants at home to the third and fourth generation, we now find the aberration of those same leading lights raucously clamoring for Libya to be invaded or Serbia to be bombed. The play may have changed, the important thing is to be on stage!

Take the Gulf War. It would be interesting to analyze how a man like Bush—certainly nobody's paragon of moral probity or intellectual finesse—managed to bamboozle a gaggle of European intellectuals into baying for Arab blood.

The general attitude seems to be: let us construct a tight Europe, let us build a wall around our accumulated privileges and keep out the hungry and the dirty and the poor. We're all right, Jack; it is an idealist delusion to be concerned about those to the South and the East of us. And this at a time when roads in Europe are again clogged with refugees, when the notion of "ethnic purification" has once more reared its hoary head, while Africans trying to sneak into the paradise of paler skins are drowning in the Gibraltar Straits.

No wonder that so many writers have withdrawn to the campuses, there like alienated baboons to deconstruct, to eviscerate and sniff at the innards of our art—the phonemes and the signifiers.

Or let us consider Africa. A few months ago I finished writing an African journal. In the process I came across the *Large Illustrated Description of Africa* by Olfert Dapper, published in Amsterdam in 1668. In it are to be found the most outlandish descriptions of exotic animals such as the unicorn, or another with the body of a wolf and a man's legs, and of tribes that walk on their heads with the feet in the air, or also others with their mouths and eyes in their bellies. The thought struck me that to the world at large Africa has always been a dark hinterland of the psyche, perforce unexplored, a sunken continent of the unknown or the subconscious upon which to project all the delicious fantasies of magic and death. An updated variation of this fabulation is, to the outside world, the depiction of present-day Africa as a continent where dying is a mass pastime, best left alone to its starvation, desertification, tribal wars, AIDS, and the implosion of its social structures.

In the South generally—under this generic term I refer to the so-called peripheral world when compared to the rich northern countries, to those areas of our planet where the majority of mankind live and die, also known as the developing or emergent or Third World—in the South, then, the activities of writing and politics often are more complementary than they would appear to be in the North. One reason for this must be that the struggle for dignity against an unfair power balance is closely intertwined with cultural resistance. Politics there still crackle with basic existential needs, including striving to revalorize or shape a cultural identity that has been humiliated. This incidentally is the easy part, if painful: to resist, to point a finger at history and at the hyenas across the border, to fight vested injustices. The difficulties come when we have to imagine viable alternatives, when we realize that the ends do not justify the means, when we see that the troubles are caused by our weaknesses rather than the strength of the hereditary exploiters. The unease also comes when we observe that our noble writers, fattened on protest, are as adept as their northern counterparts at becoming scheming and demagogic politicians.

I do not intend to denigrate the importance of African writers bringing to the attention of a wider audience the history and aspirations and complex cultures of our continent. But I have sat in on too many gatherings where all the old litanies of being victims are trundled out, laced with the posturing of pseudorevolutionaries bearding northern sensitivities. I too wallowed in the trough of self-pity. Often I think that the weaker we are, the more eloquent our protest becomes. Mostly though, these are stratagems for blackmailing the North's bleeding heart for conscience money. So often, for example, do we bewail the fact of being dispossessed of our native tongues. And yet I know of very few African writers willing to get stuck in the task of establishing networks of publishing, distribution, and education in indigenous languages. I don't see us creating the facts on the ground, counting on our own abilities, and sharing these with the disinherited populations who find themselves arbitrarily subjected to the rip-off structures called "independent states" from which only the elite few or the military many benefit. The sad fact is that African writers, by choice or out of necessity or alienation, write for non-African readers.

And so on to South Africa. I intimated at the outset of my paper that I find myself nowhere now. It is true that I have been back to that no man's land, but I soon found that I couldn't fit in, that I could neither condone the conversions of those who switched overnight from being privileged members of the master class to pen-carriers for the liberators (without missing a goosestep, as it were), nor continue unquestioningly supporting, in the name of "unity" the cause I helped struggle for. "Unity in the face of the enemy," I found, was the strategy exerted to establish a new hegemony of mediocrity where the notion of quality, for example, was decried as "bourgeois irrelevant." The fragrance of revolution had been blown away by the stench of politics.

Only natural, you might say: the naive dreaming had to be put to rest. But I had hoped that we could grasp and carry forward the vision of our uniqueness posited on the incredibly rich diversity of origins and modes of expression, that we could decisively rally around our purity, which is a profound *métissage* of cultures, and that this would enable us to reach out to the worlds of Africa and Europe and the East even. National reconciliation could be effected, I thought, on condition that there's no white-out of memory, provided, I said, that we break open the silences, that we get all the repressed *non-dits* out in the open.

It was not to be. Why not? To my mind there are many reasons. By the time the liberation movements were allowed again to operate legally inside the country, and the exiles permitted to return, two essential dimensions of our dreamspace had caved in—"virtual socialism" had collapsed, and "national liberation" on the African model, so it turned out, had led to disastrous misery nearly everywhere. (It must be said that the West did next to nothing to help the poor suckers build a viable and defendable alternative dispensation. Could it be because consumerism is the only western ideology offered for sale, with arms and munitions and the attendant high-tech toys as surplus currency with which to open the markets, and thus that the only example proposed would be democratic death on the hire purchase system?)

We had become flabby and arrogant in exile, spoilt like harem women on the sweetmeats of international support. Wasn't our cause the moral basket case of the world? Exiles talking about the plight of their situation and of the suffering back home, you must know, are like fish learning to breathe on dry land—there will be much gasping and heaving, but ultimately we are only that: fish on dry land. Now the international community suddenly lost interest. They found other fish to fry. Ethnicity came back into fashion, the break-up of states became plausible. Africa was written off, and we were now part of Africa.

For too long had we lied to others and to ourselves—and most criminally to those struggling and waiting inside—in the name of mobilization, about the extent of the "armed struggle," about how well we had thought through and prepared for the future, about the nature of our alliances and the excellence of our internal democracy. For too long, in fact, did we put off the need for democratization. And we had learned too much from the enemy, hoping to steal their power by imitation, adopting their ruthless and autocratic and secretive ways. We made the townships ungovernable, and now they are and remain indeed ungovernable.

And in the initial euphoria we misread the situation. The state had never given up on their war against the population. War continued in the name of peace; it is spreading its poison and destruction still. We underestimated the commitment of state securocrats to leave a scorched earth to the future. Worst of all, human life had been made too cheap. Now, with the incumbent government fanning the fires, pitching group against group, dislocating the black community, the slaughtering has attained its own momentum. Who can ever rule again without repression?

The ongoing filthy war in South Africa is, to my mind, not so much about a centralized and unified majority-ruled state on the one hand, as opposed to a federal dispensation with decentralized power—no, it is (or ought to be) about the devolution of power and the sharing of responsibilities. It is about the contours and conflicts and cutting edges and tangent planes between State and civil society. When there's a conflation (willed by politicians) of State and Party, State and workers, State and culture, State and ideology—then you have a dictatorship, be it of the Party (supposedly on behalf of the urban and rural proletariat), or the military, or an elite, or an individual. Under those circumstances the citizen becomes what George Konrad called a *Staatsmensch*, somebody who has integrated the notion of himself as pawned possession and expression of the State.

In South Africa the State belongs to the Broederbond (a fraternal semisecret society of the male white Afrikaner elite), laying claim to it in the name of the history and the interests of a narrowly defined ethnic and cultural group, the Afrikaners, and farmed out to thick-headed administrators, cruel and cowardly securocrats, rapacious captains of our capitalism of the primitive colonial kind. Of course the Afrikaner state is built on sand—we're neither racially "pure" nor culturally homogeneous or exclusive—and all the spilled blood did not consolidate the foundations. At present, members of the African National Congress elite—directed by its own Broederbond, the South African Communist Party—are being co-opted by or otherwise infiltrating the State. The Party is investing the terrains of trade unionism, culture, and higher education, to gather the captives for the unaltered State which will in future be denoted as "democratic," "united," and "of the people." So far the ANC has been allowed to sidestep the contradictions between nationalism and democracy in a multinational state simply because the democratically correct objective of "majority rule" brings with it the unspoken inevitability of black rule. In the meantime, racism continues unabated, no longer needing laws to bolster the structures and practices of iniquity. Social and economic dissolution may have reached the point of no return.

If I insist upon this conundrum (to be found in different declensions all over Africa), it is because I believe we can only save ourselves by strengthening the democratic capacities of civil society (the trade unions, cultural groupings, the media, citizens' associations); by vigorously confining politicians to their rule as servants of the community, counteracting their "natural" tendency for feeding off society's labor to pollute and corrupt us with their arrogant power (some riches are after all still *produced* and not just stolen from the beggar's hat of speculation); and especially by recognizing the State for what it is—our necessary cancerous cyst that must be kept under control by a judicious mixture of combat and care.

I believe that such a "permanent revolution," this harmony of dynamic change (where the deontologies and responsibilities of the various groupings will be constantly assessed and buttressed, by hook or by crook), is not a "luxury" as thinking Africans sometimes aver, but a staple necessity for public hygiene. I should also say that my conception of the State (and therefore of power to the people) does not flow from a liberal tradition, but grows from some half-forgotten yearnings of the left. In this vision, I think, the State (ultimately the homeland of politicians) will be a defined and picketed organism, as democratically controlled and accountable as possible, guaranteeing the separation of powers, mediating conflicting interests, using its accumulated assets as repository of the common good to provide protection for the weak and to promote social justice for all. ¡Nada más!

We all saw the light at the end of the tunnel before the roof caved in. Or, as a sad poet put it: the shit has hit the fan, but it doesn't matter—the fans don't work anymore.

Did History finally devour Imagination? Is it true then that nothing can ever grow again on the killing fields? What about the writers? I found, by and large, two categories: those who know but do not speak up, tongue-tied by guilt or a false sense of solidarity; the others who believe that repeating the mumbo-jumbo of slogans constitutes revolutionary literature. And then there are those, the commissars who never wrote, or only incidentally, who now run the "structures" of "cultural workers." Too many writers believe they have their noses pointing towards fragrant promises of the republic of peace just over the hill, when they are in fact locked in on slipstreams from the comfortable and perfumed buttocks of politicians digging for power to the Party.

When I pointed this out—and I could have been wrong as so often before, how much I still hope to be proven wrong!—comrades asked: "Why can't you be happy now that we've won?" Former friends accused me of being a bird of doom (and perhaps of ill omen), coming periodically to shit all over the beloved country before returning to my comfortable perch abroad. Newspaper editors admonished me to stop whining so as not to scare the children, and to go away to the luxury of so-called exile. Anonymous readers, freed at last to show what they thought all along of the smug moral magistrate, wrote to say: "Fuck you! Fuck you good!"

So where does that leave me? Where do I stand? What is my politics? It may shock you when I say I find this personal tabula rasa, this zero degree of functionality, exhilarating.

This is what I have learned: It is better to be writing and painting than to be mind-sucked by television's gospel of stupidity. Nobody ever said that suffering leads to wisdom, or tolerance; but not being able to express terror leads to new permutations of terror. Writing may be a lie, but it is a small one compared to the big lie of politics. Even ivory towers need central heating. Put a human being in a position of power and he or she will abuse it instantly, or soon after. Commitment of the artist to the evolution of ethics is not a choice, it is a breathing, a rhythm, because it partakes of creation. Writing will be political because it incarnates a ceaseless struggle with the resistant and approximate matter of perceptual awareness, and because this struggle will mouth in shared codes, and is thus social. Writing, which is writing the self and rewriting the world, is best at home in civic society. There is a dialectical relationship between "repeating the known" as a way of flexing the sense of belonging, and inventing the private road of individuality with madness as end.

Politics is a power trip, but no longer the dominant factor among the other powers, such as (not exhaustively): the Mafia, the media, the empires of drugs, the arms dealers, the banks, the multinationals, the academics, the administrations, the armies, the security establishments. . . . Language is the memory of power and memory is the power of pain. The State is a blind mirror that will steal your face. Writing that aims for the transforming awareness can be about searching (for) the margins to stretch the limits; politics however moves down the center from compromise to collusion to corruption.

At last we know that not all problems need to have solutions, because some solutions can be more disastrous than the problems. Politics may be as much of a fiction as writing is. Everywhere we look, we see the implosion of public morals. Socialists are even more greedy for protocol and patronage than conservatives are. Every North needs a South (it may even fabricate an internal one, as we see happening in Europe now), if only to provide for the movement of disequilibrium.

The nature of man is bestial, the concept of progress futile and redundant, but struggle for decency continues. There will always be history because there will always be dreaming, and therefore conflict. No gain is permanent, and permanence is not a gain either. It is the walking that life is all about; the goal is only a certain dimension or configuration of absence that will help to elicit activity. Knowing meaning is a good way of preparing the unknowing. To tell a story is to activate a dream.

I must keep running after myself so as not to lose sight of the dark light of creativeness: that is, subverting the hegemony, unhinging the seemingly unstoppable process of accretion and accumulation, rattling the skeleton and the empty bowl of the mind, taunting that powdered death called Respectability, keeping the cracks whistling, fighting for revolution against politics. Aesthetics and ethics cannot be separated.

It is important to take responsibility for the story: Imagination is politics. He who travels alone, travels fastest, but in the company of friends you go further . . .

Panel Discussion
Panelists: Marc Chénetier, Nuruddin Farah,
William H. Gass, William Matheson, Steven Meyer

William H. Gass: I must say that I find the optimism of this paper reassuring. I'm sincere about that; it suggests to me that a clear eye is still possible. There are many points raised by this presentation which I think moves to the very heart of our subject, and I suppose it's about time we got there. I'd like to suggest that we begin by turning our attention to the nature of power itself. This has underlaid a lot of what has been said already; it's certainly fundamental as I listened to Breyten's talk. Do we, for example, as writers, really want power? We often moan about our utility, our impotence, our lack of readers, lack of response, our inability to get things done, not only as citizens of the world where we at least have, presumably in this country, the right to cast a ballot. But writing isn't the same as casting a ballot. Suppose, as happens in evil stories, we were to get our wish. Suppose we could cause things to come about as we imagine. Suppose our words really caused motion in the limbs of our readers. Nuruddin, do you want to begin?

Nuruddin Farah: No, I was waiting . . . oh, all right. I find the paper rather weak. It is full of generalizations, with subheadings strung together with semicolons. I'll explain myself. Breyten says: "I have no recognizable politics in any accepted sense." He also says, "Friends accuse me of being a bird of doom and perhaps of ill omen, coming"—to Africa, that is—"periodically to shit all over the country before returning to my comfortable perch outside."

Breyten Breytenbach: No, coming to South Africa.

Nuruddin Farah: Yes, South Africa. So you see, one of the things that Breyten spends a great deal of time on is what African writers, who happen to be represented here today by him and myself, do with regard to publishing and writing. Writers wherever they are in the world today, whether they are in Africa or in North America, are at the mercy of publishing houses, commercialization, and the commoditization of the publishing world. Regardless of what the African writer does, there is no point in talking about publishing because even in America the majority of the authors have difficulty finding good publishers interested in publishing good literary works. We were told yesterday that Amiri Baraka has difficulty finding publishers. For Breyten to complain about the fact that African writers do not pay any attention to where their works are published or do not organize themselves enough to do that, I find a bit unreasonable.

Something else that we've heard oftentimes, and from Breyten, is that politicians are corrupt. I would be interested in addressing ourselves to the question, why is it that politics is corrupt, and what happens to writers when they move into the arena of politics? Do they remain clean, pure?

Another point that I'd like to make is that Breyten says that he believes writing is about traveling, not about reaching a destination. Is Breyten the kind of writer who lives in Europe, goes to Africa, travels to get enough material out of Africa, writes a book about it, and then comes back? Is this what Africa means for him?

(Long pause)

Marc Chénetier: If Breyten won't respond, could I try in his place?

Breyten Breytenbach: I thought I'd do it once we've gone around.

Marc Chénetier: Could I have a go at it?

Breyten Breytenbach: Sure.

Marc Chénetier: While I have the microphone, I'd like to say, because it's the last time we'll meet together, that I'm extremely happy that this went on as it did. There's been more brought to us during this conference than in a long time in my memory. This conversation would be impossible if the general atmosphere was not what it was.

I would like to go in the opposite direction Nuruddin took, not because I disagree with him necessarily, but I think there is another way of looking at Breyten's paper. I don't think your definition of the paper is exact—or if it is, it is a compliment. One doesn't have to be an expert in the martial arts to know that transforming a position of weakness into strength or taking advantage of the power and onrush of the opponent is a very good way of proceeding. I think that Breyten's paper was strong proportionately to the fact that he had acquired the power to describe it as weak. To me this is really the essence in any conversation that wants to be far from the political forum, which this is not. I was particularly sensitive to the emphasis that Breyten put on process. I think this is crucial to what we're discussing and probably the only thing that will allow us to make sense of any relation between writing and politics. I think it was Barrett Watten, an American poet, who said, "The train always reinvents the station." It is in this idea of process, which Antonio Skármeta and Luisa Valenzuela talked about yesterday, that I would like to find a way out of this predicament.

Antonio, you will remember, described democracy as that which remains open and is the avowal of weakness and imperfection. This is where its richness lay. It was important to me, because I thought writing had the function of keeping things unconcluded. He described democracy as that which is not utopian, nonteleological. We were discussing the possibility of writing remaining nonteleological to remain efficient, not closing upon itself. To take two very different spheres of speech—we are in the midst of a presidential campaign right now and we hear opponents accuse each other of waffling, but I think waffling is of the order here. If we don't waffle, we've had it.

There is, in the history of poetry in this century, a great number of avowals of defeat. They are the testimony. When Pablo Neruda says that the metaphor is hopelessly powerless, he makes the sentence "The blood of children can only run like the blood of children" extraordinarily powerful. When Vladimir Mayakovsky, obliged to go propagandizing, suddenly discovers the worth of the self-apparent word and decides "to put his heel on the throat of his song," he becomes Mayakovsky. Failure in this area is power. Waffling in this context would be the refusal to be secure in one's convictions. If the individual is not more intelligent than the group, and if the writer is not more intelligent than any other individual, he may be more agile in the footwork that is necessary to get out from under the pall of certainty.

I left a rather active life in politics because it was a rut in which you could not make what mattered to you move fast enough. The structure always petrified before it had achieved its aim. It is extremely problematic. Valéry, in a wonderful essay called *L'Idée fixe*, says that it is an extraordinary idea that people should have fixed ideas because an idea is precisely that which is not fixed. An idea is that which waffles. I'd like to commend Breyten's paper for exemplifying within itself, as the product of a true poet should, what he meant. The contradictions in his paper did not weaken it. They illustrated that attempt at finding a way forward. Process was illustrated by that paper. So getting out of the rut of his own classifications that were so rigid in the beginning was the very way in which one could demonstrate that you cannot as a writer, as a poet concerned with the political process, insist on anything but the word process in the political process.

William H. Gass: Thank you, Marc. I think that one of the things that has been going on in this conference from the beginning is that at least two senses of politics have been swimming side by side—or I should say, one is the fish and the other the ocean. One notion of politics is that everything is political. It's impossible to, you know, wipe your nose. There goes a Kleenex, there's more economics and that's more trees and so on and so forth. All of that is, in this broadest sense of politics, true. When Breyten says he has achieved a position—and I think it's an achievement—of not having a politics, I think what he means is an ideological stance, a set of beliefs and ideas that tell him in advance what to think, which then make it possible not to investigate something freshly, clearly, and without bias, to achieve a position in which you are freeing your mind. This is the problem that politicians have always had with writers. A writer has to see all around the subject. A writer has to be able to penetrate any particular position: something presenting itself as a vice, something presenting itself as a virtue, and the other elements. If there's time, I may return to my investigation of the virtues, as I'm working on a paper in which I try to prove that every virtue contains seven vices. But now let's turn to Steven.

Steven Meyer: Nuruddin and Breyten gave a reading on Monday evening. Breyten read from the text he refers to here, a chapter in which he discusses returning to his dying father. What moved me wasn't so much the explicit portrait of this but that there were two catalogues, one at the beginning and one at the end of this chapter. He seems to be traveling in different directions. They're all names of places—correct me if I'm wrong—and the first list incorporates all the various languages that one can find still being spoken in South Africa. By the end of the chapter, after his father has died, the list that concludes the chapter has, I think, only place names in Afrikaans. I understand that you gave up Afrikaans as a language for poetry when you were released from prison. The lists struck me as poetry in Afrikaans, so this gesture is enormously complicated. You talked about how African writers "bewail the fact of being dispossessed of our native tongues," and you complain that this is too easy a response. What is the nature of the interrelation of the languages in South Africa? American writers from the end of the eighteenth century throughout the nineteenth century and into the twentieth had a problem, which is how to continue what began as a revolution in the language of the oppressor. The American language as a literary tongue took a great deal of time to develop. The possibility of a literary politics was questioned given the fact that almost all the writers at the time of the revolution were politicians. The problem with teaching American literature of that period is that they're all politicians.

Breyten Breytenbach: When Marc was speaking I remembered the saying, "What is a mind for if you cannot change it?" which, of course, is double-edged. In the process of writing, one is also writing one's self. Bill pointed out that one goes into this action never totally cold, never totally pure, never totally unprepared, but at least poised towards the possibility of ending up where you didn't think you were going to be when you went in, leaving yourself that chance—in all kinds of ways. This has been spoken about over the last few days, how in the process of writing something may emerge that you didn't expect. This is true also if writing is, as it is for me, a means towards understanding. I must interact with that means of understanding. Writing opens up the possibility for understanding to me, and I want to use it accordingly. I cannot, beforehand, expect that that means will bring only a certain kind of understanding. That, of course, is one of the essential differences between writing and politics.

But I first want to get back to the language question. And then perhaps just one or two words to the issues raised by Nuruddin. At the moment in South Africa the situation is as follows: there are two official languages, English and Afrikaans. You may remember in 1976 there was a very big uprising in the townships called the Soweto riots, which was sparked off by resistance of the schoolchildren to being obliged to read or to learn Afrikaans. They didn't want to be taught in Afrikaans, as it was seen and depicted as the language of the masters, the judges, the policeman, the prison warden, the military. How many people speak Afrikaans and how many people speak English? One always has to handle these statistics very carefully because there is a self-serving element for those who produce them. It is claimed, though, that probably the largest single linguistic group in the country are those who speak Zulu. It would seem then, that afterwards come Afrikaans speakers at something like 19 percent of the population of the country. Now the white population (the Afrikaners) only constitutes something like 8 percent of the population. So it's clear that there's a very large number of people beyond the so-called Afrikaner community who speak Afrikaans as a first language. This is true, for instance, for 80 percent of the so-called colored people. Colored people in South Africa are the people who are of supposedly mixed descent, the results of intermarriage between Europeans, Khoi people who have disappeared, African people, and slaves brought from other parts of the world. There's a fair percentage of African people, Black African people, in the Free State, who are Sotho speakers and who also speak Afrikaans. Furthermore, it is true that in the townships on the reef, in Soweto and in other parts, you'll come across a form of Afrikaans that is called Fleitau, which is very heavily based in Afrikaans. Afrikaans, as I tried to explain in *The True Confessions of an Albino Terrorist*, is a creole language. It grew from a number of seventeenth-century Dutch dialects before Dutch was one official language, *Algemeen Beschaafd Nederlands* (The Queen's Dutch), as it became since then. In fact the two have since developed in quite opposite directions. They share probably 60 percent of the vocabulary, so you can trace a shared vocabulary, with adaptations. Afrikaans had another substratum which is very important, what we call Malay Portuguese, a seamen's language, a kind of lingua franca spoken all down the African coast and all the way up again into parts of the Far East, wherever the Dutch and Portuguese sailors and others went. You also have another element, Malay, brought over by slaves from the other Dutch colonial possessions at the time. So the grammatical structure of Afrikaans is like Malay, it's nothing like a European language. Then Afrikaans took about 40 percent of its vocabulary from all kinds of other languages including indigenous ones. I mentioned to someone the other day the Afrikaans word for a chameleon, *trapsoetjies*, meaning "walk softly," is a translation for the Xhosa word for a chameleon, "he who walks softly." There are also examples of how forms of speech and the importance given to certain elements of the language, such as alliteration, rhythm, and repetition have been carried over into Afrikaans. All of these make up Afrikaans, which took off from there and showed a fairly recognizable creole characteristic of inventiveness, of using the diminutives, for example. All this means that Afrikaans is in fact a language made not by the whites. For two centuries the whites thought they were not speaking Afrikaans, which they called "kitchen Dutch." In fact it was spoken by people who had no European language, who took over what they could of the language of the master and mixed it with all kinds of other languages. Afrikaans is a colored language, a bastard language, a product of *métissage*. In that sense it is emblematic of other things that took place in the country. Afrikaans has to a large extent, since the 1970s and 1980s, been won back, been recuperated by its original creators. It was used for purposes of contestation and to expand the awareness of the people using it. It is taught at all levels, not only among whites but among the so-called coloreds, too. So in a sense now there is no longer any stigma attached to Afrikaans.

I'm misquoted when it's said I was never going to write in Afrikaans again. I protested against the way it was being imposed on other people, a kind of official Afrikaans. I predicted that if this continued then Afrikaans would die; it would become a language for tombstones only. This has not happened. I never stopped writing in Afrikaans. I could never write poetry in any other language besides Afrikaans. I don't think one has a choice, at least I don't, in the language in which one writes. It's the one that comes to me most intimately, the most spontaneously, the most intuitively. It need not be the one you know the best. I have a suspicion that possibly I know English better or even French better than I know Afrikaans by now; I've been living away from Afrikaans for too many years. But it's still the one that wells up automatically whenever that poem has to happen. I sometimes compare it to drawing, when you want to get something on paper immediately, that intimate relationship between what you observe and what you want to say, that for me would be Afrikaans. When I paint it is in English or in French. That's my own private metaphor.

What's going to happen to Afrikaans? The African National Congress has proposed that there should be acceptance of all languages spoken in the country, because there are many languages, of which English is one. English, surprisingly enough, is not considered to be the first language by very many people in the country. It only comes after Zulu, Afrikaans, Xhosa, then English, slightly before Sotho, for instance, and then come the others like Venda and Tswana. Now the ANC has proposed that all of these languages ought to have official status, at least regionally, but that we should perhaps accept that we are going to have one lingua franca that will have to be English. That's probably what's going to happen. What's going to happen to Afrikaans if it loses its official status? Some people point out that once a language is no longer used for decree, at court, or at certain levels of scientific research, or in teaching, its usefulness shrinks. This may well be the case. I don't know. Does it mean that many people who are now not writing in their own language will start writing in Zulu? That may very well happen. People have resisted that because the government—which is still in power—had as its previous policy what we called Bantustan education, and that implied that each ethnic group, each linguistic group, was supposed to use its own language. It was to emphasize the fact that there was no majority, that the whites were one minority among all other minorities. That's one way of trying to wish away basic mathematics. So there was resistance among black writers to use Sotho or Zulu or Tswana. There's an ongoing debate about this.

Let me just say something about your remarks, Nuruddin. I would agree with you, yes, it's a weak paper. In fact, I'm very proud of it being a weak paper. I'd be a little bit worried if, at this stage in my life, I wrote strong papers. I've been leading myself by the nose strongly in many directions, and I'd rather sit back a bit and see it coming. If you say it's weak stylistically, quite specifically, well thank you, I'll go back and try to sort it out. You say I mentioned I have no politics. I said no recognizable politics. Then I go on to contradict that by ending up identifying elements that may be more a mixture of convictions, assumptions, and awarenesses—elements forming something one may call politics, because certainly for me it translates into definite positions from time to time. I know, for instance, when I criticize certain things I don't agree with, it is informed by, among others, some of the things I mentioned there. So of course I have a politics. But I did try to say, perhaps not clearly enough, that in a sense I felt myself an impostor here, because I was invited as a writer with a politics. I thought, well, people probably expect me to come with a recognizable politics, and I'm not sure whether I would want that particular kind of clear politics at the moment, to which Bill referred to quite correctly as ideology or partisanship in the strict narrow political sense.

About African publishing—well, yes, obviously, I generalize a lot. In fact, someone like Ngũgĩ has tried to revive the need, respectability, and usefulness of writing in his own language and to make it possible to be published in that language. There are many exceptions to this. But I still believe that it is up to us to change the situation. I'm not suggesting for a single moment that we must turn our backs on the possibilities of being published by proper publishing houses. I think we must at least put in as much energy in trying to get off the ground the possibilities of publishing, distributing, making accessible, through translations or other means, the works that we are involved in on the continent itself. In a very schematic way of looking at it, I see that you have educated elites who nearly always use a foreign language. It may be a universal language, like English or French, but it is foreign, the ex-colonial language. You have underneath that a vast majority of people, probably 80 percent if not more, who do not know those languages, and thereby, in a sense, are not pooled into any form of political process. They can't go to meetings and express themselves. They probably can't even read if they were asked to vote. It's a matter of using language, making it possible for people to achieve the capacity for participating in their own lives through the language that they use. That's what I was trying to say. I happen to be involved with some friends in doing something like that, from Dakar, Senegal, and into Mali, working with a small publishing house there, trying to make it possible to find a good, helpful charitable European concern that could advance us money to make it possible to print and publish works in the local languages there, to try to get it out to the people. Then the last point, well, I don't think you seriously intended to say that, because I take it as a deep—

Nuruddin Farah: What was the point?

Breyten Breytenbach: Going to Africa from time to time and sucking out a little of the exoticism and going back. I spend half of my time in Africa. I've done so for the last few years. I probably would have done so more had it been possible before. We don't need to go into details about that. The way I look, I could probably sneak in on any European context, but since 1960, since I first left South Africa, I've never been able to feel European. I try to help to create the possibilities to make it possible to spend more time there. And that's where it's at.

Nuruddin Farah: My major problems have more to do with the fact that you accused me yesterday of depending so much on the international world's public opinion support. And yet, what you're trying to do now is to start a publishing house with the help of European money, one; two, you say that we Africans continue to sing the litanies of being victims. Now it is possible that you haven't been reading some of the books coming out of Africa. The generation of Africans to which I belong have insisted that the problem lies with us, not with the outside world, and that we must serve our interests in our own way, without help from outside, without being dependent on others. With regard to writers writing in languages, whatever the language is, and without making a finer point out of a very dull one, I should like to say that if you go to Oxford, Mississippi, and you give William Faulkner's novels to people walking in the street and you say to them, "This is your son, can you read the book?" how many people in Oxford, Mississippi, can read and understand what Faulkner has written? Take Joyce—what?

Marc Chénetier: —or in St. Louis.

Nuruddin Farah: —or in St. Louis. Well, I didn't want to be thrown out immediately. So the question of audience is irrelevant. The audience of a writer is any person, regardless of any continent or country where the author may be read. There is politics in the pushing and promoting of certain languages, especially in the context of southern Africa, because the apartheid regime insisted that Africans should write in their languages and not in English, you see? So any person who now says that Africans in South Africa should write in an African language may sound suspect—I know that it doesn't so far as you're concerned. I might accuse you of being naive and all that, but not being unhealthy, too.

Breyten Breytenbach: —of being evil. That reminds me of the very first poem I wrote that was ever published: "He doesn't know what he's doing/have mercy on him."

Nuruddin Farah: I heard your paper, I didn't read it—and it said to me that, on the one hand, you turn the world into a turf that belongs to you as an educated, intellectual, cosmopolitan living in Paris three months of the year, three months in Spain, and four months in Senegal. But whenever you turn to Africa, your comments do not seem to be informed by an understanding of the world in which you live. When I talked to Bill Gass about publishing he said, "Big publishers tend to pulp or remainder books, whereas small publishing houses tend to have a personal relationship with the author." The same problem occurs in Africa. Writers have difficulty finding a publisher who would bring out good-looking books that are available anywhere and that may be bought by practically everybody. What I'm suggesting you do is that you think about the context in which you live, the European context, in Paris or Madrid, and apply the same logic to the comments you are making about Africa. Now another thing is that in Africa not many things function, nothing functions—

Breyten Breytenbach: Well, let's try and do something about it.

Nuruddin Farah: That's what we're doing. That's why I live in Africa. To say that there are other things that are wrong with Africa and to isolate only a few cases is not to see the whole. I mean you're concentrating on minor imperfections, whereas I'm saying, let's deal with the major imperfections—

Breyten Breytenbach: I remember being in Lagos a few years ago with Wole Soyinka. A general was sitting next to him on the podium saying, "Let us commit ourselves to making sure that before the end of the century no country in Africa will be ruled by a military regime." We're nearly there now. I would suggest that's one of the major things wrong with large aspects of Africa, the fact that we're still ruled by military regimes. So I don't think these are small things.

Nuruddin Farah: Does that mean that there's something wrong with America because Bush is the president?

William H. Gass: Certainly.

Breyten Breytenbach: Of course, yes.

William H. Gass: I would like to—

Breyten Breytenbach: We will halt this but just one thing. I did not intend to suggest that African authors ought to publish in African languages or in Africa or with African publishers exclusively, or even occasionally. What I did try to suggest, was that African authors, being people who have that kind of understanding and who are concerned about the implications, should help to make it possible for publication to take place. I'm not suggesting necessarily your books or my books, or anybody else's. If that can also happen, so much the better. But to extend the infrastructure that would make it possible to have access to literature. I think writers have a very big role in that. That is all I wanted to say.

Nuruddin Farah: Just one small point. When you suggest that we do this then it means that we are not only working on publishing but also on many different facets of the problem.

Breyten Breytenbach: Of course.

William H. Gass: I'd like to turn this over to the audience.

Audience Member: I must ask you as a writer, not as a politician, to address some tremendously emotional issues. First, we don't hear people talking about the sincerity or insincerity of De Klerk. From what we get from the media—not just here but the world media—this man seems like he must be sincere. If not he would be on the other side of what he is proposing. At the same time, no one talks of "one person, one vote," something very central to the issue. I don't hear writers discussing this, and it's at the very heart of what is going on—not what Chief Buthelezi and Mandela, the Zulus and Inkatha or the Afrikaners are doing. It brings to mind slavery. Then there is Sharpeville. Could you talk to us as a writer, not a politician, about your feelings on whether or not this will come about again? Because over and above the unrest that's going on, the tribal conflicts, is the issue of one person, one vote.

Breyten Breytenbach: Let me start with the last one first. Could there be another Sharpeville or another massacre like that? No, I don't think there could be another massacre or an uprising because the government, be it the present one or those that will follow, will try to impose Afrikaans as a language. Nobody will want to try to impose a language any more. I think that is one lesson learned rather bloodily. I must admit I have surprisingly little feeling either way about the status of Afrikaans. I've been asked many times, sometimes subtly, sometimes very directly, to become involved in making the case for its continued existence. As I tried to explain early on, there's a recognition of who made the language, and who the people were speaking the language. Even so, I've never been able to allow myself to be mustered to defend this language. This is a kind of a natural process that will have to be sorted out very slowly by all the speakers concerned. It's certainly not part of the ANC policy—to either abolish Afrikaans or to retain it as a national language. I have to point out that the ANC documents are published in Afrikaans, English, Zulu, and Sotho. These are the four official languages used by the ANC in its meetings. There are certain areas of the country, such as the western Cape for instance where the ANC branch meetings will take place in Afrikaans only, and there may not be any white people present at all. So it's a very complicated question which I think ought to be sorted out in a natural process.

Now, as to the sincerity of De Klerk: He is not a sincere man. I tried to say in my paper that the state never ceased making war upon the population of the country. In fact, that was one of the delusions we had in the initial moments of euphoria after the February 1990 speech of De Klerk, that this meant the end of hostilities. In fact Mandela said, "This is a man of integrity and I respect his sincerity." Well, it may have been a ploy for him to say so, or wishful thinking. De Klerk has been delegated by those who put him in power to retain the privileges of that power. He's put there to assure the survival of his particular ethnic group. It can be argued, whether this is justified or not, that the majority of the people belonging to that ethnic group feel themselves threatened. It may even be argued that there could be some objective truth to it. It could be well argued that it's a possibility that South Africa is moving to a cataclysmic and final race war. There are many possibilities of what may happen over the next two years in South Africa, and nearly all of them are bloody. But whatever happens, and however he justifies doing what he's doing—and he's a very devious man, he was born into politics from grandfather, to father, to uncle, to himself—he's known as a harsh and clever politician. He's done very well from the political point of view. He's kept the ANC off balance consistently. He's got the ANC fighting from the back foot all the time. I think in the ANC we let ourselves be led into any number of dead end streets. So it's not all his being so good, it's us not getting our own act together. I don't think the man is sincere; he is pragmatic. He will not compromise an inch unless he's obliged to do so. So what we have in South Africa is a power struggle that obviates any possibility of moving towards a vision that could start taking the country forward. What we are seeing at the moment is regression, however we may try to paint it as advancing towards democracy.

Now the last point that you raised, "One man, one vote." Of course that's put forth very strongly on the programs of all the opposition parties and all the liberation movements. It's by now strongly espoused by De Klerk and his party. It all depends what you mean by one man, one vote. I think the only possible solution to having a peaceful settlement is if we really had one man, one vote, if each vote had the same weight, if that meant that it was not a crime that people could vote for representatives that would be ruling or running their lives, that these people would be held accountable, would be close to the community—but this is not what any of the parties in South Africa are about. People are concerned with gaining, through voting or other means, the legitimacy to grab hold of that power, and then settle the old scores.*

Audience Member: You claimed that you were going to make an apolitical speech. It seems to me that you defined yourself on the side of the left by your definition in a very original way. I congratulate you for that, because semantically you put three things on the side of the right that are usually attributed to the left in the United States. One of them is ecology, another is democracy, and another is intervention for human rights. Now we use those terms sacredly, talking about the death of communism, the death of socialism, as if they do not belong to the right. Could you define the right and say why you put those there?

---

*Editor's note: Nelson Mandela was sworn in as president of South Africa on May 10, 1994, after the country's first all-race election.

Breyten Breytenbach: One of the things a writer can try and do is to prod the sacred cows once in awhile and see how they move, whether they move. Nuruddin would know, coming from a country where cattle is a very precious possession. I should perhaps have put some of these things in quotation marks. But there is something serious underneath that. As you may have noticed, in the case of the intervention in the name of human rights, I put that in opposition to the confused search for justice. I'm of the opinion that if we could attain the ideal state where there would be the possibility of real justice, justice one could trust, and it would be impartial, it would be making no distinctions between people on grounds of income or sex or creed or race or whatever, then we wouldn't need human rights. Human rights has become a banner that is waved rather abusively to justify very strange things sometimes. I do not think that what's happening in the ex-Yugoslavia is really a humanitarian attempt to stop the Bosnians from dying. I think it's political maneuvering. I'm not suggesting that people shouldn't be flying in food or medicine. Of course not. Although I respect all the principles of the International Declaration of Human Rights, this has become a cop-out, at least in a way, in many of the developed countries. People, for instance, in Europe, condone the insecurity within which immigrants find themselves now, and yet they would in the name of human rights plead for intervening in another country. It may be a little of a home debate in a sense. For example, in France we debated some time ago whether there should be a mandated right to intervene for human rights, and I remember that debate was carried into the United Nations, too. And I think that becomes a very dangerous concept, because the United Nations as far as I'm concerned is an adjunct of the United States. Now what if the United States decides for its own interests it wants to intervene in a particular country? It could present that as intervening in the name of human rights.

Democracy—I would talk about that from an African point of view; it's been a bit of a buzz word, a game, something that was put forward as, "If only you can have democracy in Africa we will start giving you loads of money," or "We're going to stop giving you money until you become democratic." Now, as far as I'm concerned, democracy is not to do with a parliament sitting on top with all the structural fixtures of democracy. Yes, those are the attributes, to some extent, even the means. To me democracy is the possibility for the population, right down to every particular and at the most humble level, to become involved in their own lives. That is not really what is being meant by democracy. In a country like this only 30 percent of the people will actually vote. Yet you're voting for a type of government that is held up as the example of democracy.

The third question was about ecology. I don't want to knock ecology particularly, but you know, I am nervous of fads, of people marching and getting all excited about saving trees when people are dying. I'm not suggesting it's a choice, of course not. Obviously, these things hang together. I'm very glad that people seem to be becoming much more aware of the quality of life. We must preserve the planet and we must somehow continue living because we've got to hand it over to those coming after us. Ecology taken as a doctrine out of its context, which makes you feel good, can also serve as a means of masking a face while still allowing all kinds of other things to continue that are less good. The Maoists used to say that waving the red flag—what was the expression, to hide the revolution? or to mislead the revolution?—in other words, to hold up a banner in the name of a cause does not do much good for that particular cause. I think democracy is used that way and ecology perhaps too.

William H. Gass: Thank you, Breyten. I'm happy to conclude this panel and the conference with thanks to our speakers and panelists, who, I believe, treated our subject with utmost seriousness and made for a memorable symposium. I also want to thank our audiences for their attention, participation, and fidelity.

References

References

ARENDT, HANNAH. 1977. *Eichmann in Jerusalem*. New York: Penguin Books.

BREYTENBACH, BREYTEN. 1988. *Judas Eye and Self-Portrait/Deathwatch*. New York: Farrar, Straus & Giroux.

RICHARD, NELLY. 1992. "Cultura, politica y democracia." *Revista de Critica Cultural* 5 (July).

VALÉRY, PAUL. 1989. *The Outlook for Intelligence*. Vol. 10 of *The Collected Works of Paul Valéry*, Bollingen Series XLV. Translated by Denise Folliot and Jackson Mathews. Princeton, New Jersey: Princeton University Press.